CO-DEPENDENCY HEALING
Workbook

A Comprehensive Guide for Restoring Self-Worth, Breaking Free from Unhealthy Relationships, and Setting Healthy Boundaries

CAMERON J. CLARK

THE CO-DEPENDENCY HEALING WORKBOOK

A Comprehensive Guide for Restoring Self-Worth, Breaking Free from Unhealthy Relationships, and Setting Healthy Boundaries

© All Rights Reserved. Copyright 2023 Cameron J. Clark

ALL RIGHTS RESERVED.

No part of this book or its associated ancillary materials may be reproduced or transmitted in any form or by any means, electronic or mechanical, including photocopying, recording, or by any information storage or retrieval system without permission of publisher.

Book design by Saqib_arshad

PRINTED IN THE UNITED STATES OF AMERICA | FIRST EDITION

<u>4 FREE GIFTS!</u>

Are you ready to embark on a personal transformation journey? As a woman passionate about empowering others, I'm thrilled to offer you 4 free bonus eBooks that will propel your self-development.

By joining my email newsletter, you'll not only receive these valuable eBooks instantly but also gain access to a community dedicated to your growth. Expect personalized weekly tips, heartfelt insights, and empowering resources carefully *curated by me, Cameron J Clark.*

I believe in providing exceptional value to my community, which is why you'll also enjoy exclusive book giveaways, special discounts, and so much more. Best of all, your privacy is of utmost importance to me, and your email address is the only thing I'll ever ask for.

Don't miss out on this opportunity to invest in yourself and join a supportive community of like-minded women. Sign up today, and together, let's uncover the incredible woman within you!

To get your bonus, go to:
https://cameronjclark.com/Free-Gifts
Or scan the QR code below

- Escape the constant barrage of negative messages and take control of your thoughts.
- Transform beliefs into action: Rewire your thinking patterns to overcome self-limiting beliefs and unlock your true potential.
- Counter societal influences: Build self-acceptance, confidence, and resilience in the face of external pressures.
- Tap into ancient wisdom: Discover the timeless practice of affirmations for lasting personal transformation.
- Includes a Free Checklist as a Bonus.

Cultivate Inner Peace: Discover how acts of kindness can bring inner harmony and serenity, leading to a more fulfilling and joyful life.
- Nurture Authentic Connections: Explore how kindness fosters deeper connections with others, creating a network of support, love, and genuine relationships.
- Boost Your Well-Being: Learn how practicing kindness positively impacts your mental, emotional, and physical well-being, promoting a healthier and happier lifestyle.

- Experience Life-Changing Benefits: Discover how daily gratitude practice can bring happiness, reduce stress, improve relationships, and enhance overall well-being.
- Start a Gratitude Journal: Learn how to begin your gratitude journey by starting a journal to cultivate gratitude, shift your mindset, and invite positivity into your life.
- Deepen with Meditation: Enhance your gratitude practice through meditation, fostering inner peace, appreciation and amplifying the positive effects of gratitude in your daily life.

Harness the Power of Belief: Discover how cultivating empowering beliefs and positive thought patterns can align your mindset with manifestation, unlocking your true potential for success

- Visualization Techniques: Learn effective visualization techniques to vividly imagine and attract your desired outcomes, amplifying your manifestation abilities and bringing your dreams to life.
- Embrace Abundance Mentality: Shift from a scarcity mindset to an abundance mentality, embracing the belief that there are limitless possibilities available to you, allowing abundance to flow into your life.

Contents

INTRODUCTION — 1

What is Co-dependency? — 2
EXERCISE 1: Are You Co-dependent? — 3
Don't Worry! — 5

CHAPTER 1: THE PERILS OF A CO-DEPENDENT RELATIONSHIP — 9

EXERCISE 2: Identifying Your Relationship Patterns — 14
EXERCISE 3: What Would You Do? — 20
The Role of Negative Thoughts in Co-dependency — 22
EXERCISE 4: Challenging Negative Thoughts — 24
Let's Break it Down — 26
EXERCISE 5: Spot The Good Vs Bad Relationship — 27

CHAPTER 2: CO-DEPENDENT VS INTERDEPENDENT RELATIONSHIPS — 29

EXERCISE 6: Are You Emotionally Dependent? — 29
What About Your Relationship? — 31
Co-dependent vs Interdependent Relationships — 32
EXERCISE 7: What Do You Want? — 34
EXERCISE 8: Co-dependent or Interdependent? — 35
Are You Being Enabled? — 37
EXERCISE 9: Spot the Enabler — 41
Are You Doing the Enabling? — 42
EXERCISE 10: Are You an Enabler? — 43
How to Change Your Relationship — 44

CHAPTER 3: WHO ARE YOU? 47

Why Maintaining Your Sense of Self in a Relationship is Important 49
EXERCISE 11: I Love Myself! 51

What is Your Trigger? 52
EXERCISE 12: Identifying Your Personal Triggers 54

It's Time to Reclaim Your Power 56

Do You Need Control? 59
EXERCISE 13:Give Me Control! 60

CHAPTER 4: DON'T CROSS MY BOUNDARIES 63

EXERCISE 14:Healthy Vs. Unhealthy Expectations 65

What Do You Need in a Relationship? 68
EXERCISE 15: Let's Be Honest! 69
EXERCISE 16: What Boundaries Do You Need to Set? 70

Communicating Your Boundaries 72
EXERCISE 17: What is Your Communication Style? 73
EXERCISE 18: Spot The Boundary 75

How to Stick to Your Boundaries & What to Do if They're Crossed 77
EXERCISE 19: How Can I Communicate My Boundaries? 79

CHAPTER 5: IT'S TIME TO FOCUS ON YOU 83

EXERCISE 20: Self-Care Vs Selfishness 84

What Should You Do More Of? 86
EXERCISE 21: Give Me More! 87
EXERCISE 22: Find Some Enjoyable Things to Do 88

Recognizing Stress 88
EXERCISE 23: Are You Stressed? 91

The Art of Saying "No" 93
EXERCISE 24: When It's Okay to Say "No" 96

CHAPTER 6: FIVE STEPS TO BREAK FREE FROM CO-DEPENDENCY — 101

Step 1 – Recognize & Acknowledge The Problem — 101
EXERCISE 25: What's in an Emotion? — *102*

Step 2 – Truly Understand Co-dependency — 104
EXERCISE 26: Who Do You Miss? — *105*

Step 3 - Set Positive Boundaries — 105
EXERCISE 27: Pinpointing My Boundaries — *107*

Step 4 - Practice Self-Care Regularly — 108
EXERCISE 28: Do You Take Enough (Self) Care? — *109*
EXERCISE 29: Plan Your Perfect Day — *111*

Step 5 - Seeking Help & Support — 112
EXERCISE 30: How Do You Self-Soothe? — *113*

CONCLUSION — 117

EXERCISE 31: Are You Ready to Recover? — *119*

"Co-dependency is a lifestyle where you focus on meeting the needs of others while neglecting your own."

– STEVE ARTERBURN

Introduction

It's nice to do things for other people sometimes, isn't it? It gives you that warm, glowing feeling inside and you have the sensation of having done something good. You might also be happy that you've added extra points to your karma bank.

But is there a limit to how much you should do for others?

If you go around doing all the nice things for other people, when do you get time to do nice things for yourself? You need them too, you know!

You've picked up this workbook because you recognized the word 'co-dependent.' Now, you might think you are co-dependent, or you might be intrigued and want to learn more about it. Either way, we're about to join forces and go on a journey together.

Nice to meet you!

First, we need to accurately identify what co-dependency is and work out whether this is a problem in your life. After all, there's no point in learning about something that you're not totally clear on, right?

What is Co-dependency?

Co-dependency is a dysfunctional pattern of behavior in which a person relies on another person to meet their emotional and/or physical needs to the extent that they prioritize the needs of the other person over their own.

Co-dependent individuals often have low self-esteem, poor boundaries, and difficulty expressing their own needs and desires. They may feel responsible for the emotions and actions of the other person and struggle with feelings of guilt or anxiety if they are unable to meet their needs. Co-dependency can occur in any type of relationship, including romantic partnerships, friendships, and family relationships.

Co-dependency can be damaging for several reasons.

First, it can lead to an unhealthy and unbalanced relationship dynamic, where one person is overly reliant on the other person for their emotional well-being. This can create a sense of obligation or pressure on the other person, who may feel responsible for meeting the co-dependent person's needs.

Second, co-dependency can lead to a loss of individuality and personal identity. The co-dependent person may prioritize the needs of the other person over their own, neglecting their own interests, hobbies, and goals. This can lead to a loss of self-esteem and sense of purpose.

Third, co-dependency can prevent personal growth and development. The co-dependent person may avoid confronting their own issues and problems, instead focusing on the needs of the other person. This can prevent them from developing healthy coping mechanisms and addressing their own emotional needs.

Introduction

Do you recognize yourself in any of that? If you do, don't worry, we're about to extract co-dependency from your life and bring back your personal freedom and identity. But first, how co-dependent are you, exactly?

💡 EXERCISE 1: Are You Co-dependent?

This quiz will give you a definitive answer on whether you're co-dependent, and it will give you some clues as to how much work you need to do to change your life.

After all, if you don't know your journey's starting point, it's going to be very hard to navigate your way through the rest of it.

Answer each question with "Yes" or "No".

1. Do you often find yourself putting the needs of others before your own needs and desires?

Yes / No

2. Do you feel responsible for the emotions and actions of others, even when they are not your fault?

Yes / No

3. Do you have difficulty expressing your own thoughts, feelings, and needs to others?

Yes / No

4. Do you feel guilty or anxious when you say "no" to someone else's requests or needs?

Yes / No

5. Do you have a hard time making decisions without seeking the approval or input of others?

Yes / No

6. Do you often feel like you need to be in a relationship to feel complete or happy?

Yes / No

7. Do you struggle with setting and maintaining boundaries with others?

Yes / No

8. Do you often feel like you are "walking on eggshells" around others, trying to avoid conflict or upsetting them?

Yes / No

9. Do you have a tendency to enable others, even when it is not in your best interest?

Yes / No

10. Do you feel like you have lost a sense of who you are, or have difficulty identifying your own interests and values?

Yes / No

Scoring: Give yourself one point for each "Yes" answer. You don't get any points for "No."

- **0-2 points:** You are likely not co-dependent and have a healthy sense of self.

- **3-6 points:** You may have some co-dependent tendencies and could benefit from focusing on your own needs and developing healthy boundaries.

- **7-10 points:** You may have a significant issue with co-dependence and could benefit from extra help to address these patterns of behavior.

Don't Worry!

> "You are not required to set yourself on fire to keep other people warm."
>
> – UNKNOWN

The point of this quiz isn't to make you feel bad. It's to give you an idea of your situation. If you find that you are quite co-dependent, the first thing to do is accept it and realize that you needs to change.

You'll never have a healthy relationship if you're always doing everything for the other person and neglecting yourself. Repeat after me – I MATTER TOO!

The longer you remain co-dependent, the more damage you'll do to your self-esteem, and the longer you might stay in a relationship that does you no good.

So, what do you want to get out of this workbook? Scribble some notes down below and then when you reach the end of the book, review this section to see if your expectations were met.

Remember, you must be honest with yourself in all the exercises in this book. There is nothing to be ashamed of here; by embracing your co-dependence, you can do something about it. But if you try to push it down and avoid admitting it, you'll make no progress. Do you have that much time to waste?

I didn't think so!

"Co-dependency is using a relationship to fill a bottomless void due to not feeling whole and loved as an individual."

– GRAHAM R. WHITE

Chapter 1

The Perils of a Co-dependent Relationship

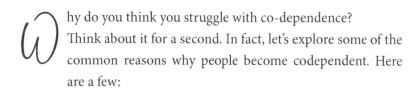

Why do you think you struggle with co-dependence? Think about it for a second. In fact, let's explore some of the common reasons why people become codependent. Here are a few:

Childhood experiences

How a child is raised has a significant impact on the type of person they will be. For children who grow up in dysfunctional families, a loving relationship is something they are not used to. The response to growing up in this environment usually goes one of two ways; they become wary of people and have a hard time trusting anyone, or they become desperate for validation, resorting to people-pleasing to feel the warmth of acceptance, no matter how fleeting.

For those in the second camp, the risk of becoming co-dependent is much higher, as they will always feel indebted to their partner for choosing them. Because of this, they will always go out of their way to give their partner everything. However, it is worth noting that dysfunction is not the only culprit. For some, co-dependency is created by the rewarding system that was present in their childhood.

In homes where the well-behaved, compliant children received compliments, treats, and attention, it is highly likely for the kids to grow up relying on others for validation. Often, they become people-pleasers, and this is kicked up a notch in romantic relationships.

Low self-esteem

For individuals with low self-esteem, their capacity for self-validation is severely limited. Their minds are always critical of who they are, their ability, and their desirability. Because of this, they always need external validation, for someone else to give them reprieve from their torturous internal talk. They always expect to be left out, and this gives the critical talk more power. So, when someone chooses them, or compliments them, the rush of happiness is unmatched.

The need for external validation drives them to do everything they can for the other person just to feel good again. They go out of their way to make the other person happier, and while the validation feels good in the moment, their low opinion of themselves eventually wins again. They get caught up in a cycle, always looking for validation, and overlooking all the negativity they endure before the next compliment hits.

People with low self-esteem are likely to hold on to their partner, always reliving the moments of validation. They use these moments to justify their attachment and blame themselves if they are criticized by their partner. They never hold anyone accountable for their actions, and always seem to give more and more to undeserving partners.

Lack of boundaries

Healthy boundaries protect us from being taken advantage of. Boundaries allow us to protect ourselves from harm in whichever form it appears. When we fail to set up healthy boundaries, we are unable to protect our interests, or even understand them. "If you don't stand for something, you'll fall for anything" is a popular quote that warns us of the dangers of being indecisive.

People who struggle with setting and maintaining healthy boundaries are highly likely to become co-dependent. Without clear boundaries, they give other people immense power over them. Because they are not focusing on their own needs, wants, and ideals, they become easily convinced that their partner has their best interest in mind, even if this is not the case. They follow along, always looking to other people to show them the way. Even in the moments where they know better, they are still easily influenced to go with what the other person deems appropriate.

Enabling behaviors

People who feel the need to rescue or fix others always feel sense of obligation or responsibility for the other person's well-being. Even as they feel sorry for the other person or plead with them to change, they always end up engaging in the more familiar enabling behavior. They get sucked in by their need to fix because they feel validated by their ability to take care of the other person.

Instead of helping, however, they get sucked into the rabbit hole. They end up in a cycle of pleas, tears, and frustration, but seem to forget it all when the other person validates their desire to be needed. However, enablers almost always fail to realize that they are co-dependent because they believe they are in control. They fail to notice that they are at the mercy of the whims of their partner, not their own desires and wants. The other person is the priority, and they are always anticipating how their partner may need them.

Cultural and societal factors

Cultural and societal factors can also contribute to the development of co-dependency. In some cultures, prioritizing the needs of others may be expected or encouraged, leading to the development of codependent tendencies. Additionally, societal messages about gender roles and expectations can also contribute to the development of co-dependency.

When individuals who give up on their own dreams for the "good of the community," or "for their families," are revered, this fosters a reliance on external validation. Self-sacrificing individuals are praised even as their needs and wants are trampled and ignored. However, the human need for acceptance and validation keeps them from choosing a different path. Life becomes about the other person, and their identity is based on their perceived value to the other person. This means that even though their self-sacrifice may be causing them harm, the alternative is scarier.

Do you recognize any of those as a possible reason for yourself? Use this space below to scribble down any experiences you can think of that might have contributed to your co-dependent nature.

....
....
....
....
....
....
....
....
....
....
....

A co-dependent relationship can never be a healthy one. You see, a healthy relationship is balanced. You both do things for one another (equally), and you spend time on your own too. You do the things you enjoy individually or with friends, and then you come together and spend time together. It gives you something to talk about!

If one person is doing all the giving and the other is taking, at some point, the giver is going to start to feel resentful, and in the end, their needs will be cast aside, never to be fulfilled. Of course, the taker is pretty happy; they're getting everything they want and need!

Not particularly healthy though, is it?

EXERCISE 2: Identifying Your Relationship Patterns

How many of the following statements do you agree with? Again, be honest and go with your gut feeling.

1. Do you often find yourself putting your partner's needs before your own?

Yes / No

2. Have you ever stayed in a relationship longer than you wanted to because you were afraid of being alone?

Yes / No

3. Do you feel responsible for your partner's emotions or well-being?

Yes / No

4. Have you ever felt like you couldn't be happy without your partner?

Yes / No

5. Do you have a hard time setting boundaries with your partner?

Yes / No

6. Have you ever felt like you were walking on eggshells around your partner?

Yes / No

7. Do you have a history of being in relationships with people who have addiction or mental health issues?

Yes / No

8. Do you often feel the need to "fix" your partner or their problems?

Yes / No

9. Have you ever compromised your values or beliefs for the sake of your relationship?

Yes / No

10. Do you tend to ignore or dismiss red flags in your relationships?

Yes / No

If you answered "yes" to several of these questions, it may be worth exploring the possibility that you have co-dependent tendencies within your relationships, now and in the past.

But don't despair! It's important to remember that co-dependency is a learned behavior, and with awareness and effort, it can be unlearned.

> Healing begins with awareness, understanding, and action."
>
> – DIANE METCALF

Let's look at some of the most common signs of co-dependence in a relationship. Place a tick next to the ones you recognize as your behavior patterns.

- **Difficulty setting boundaries:**
  For co-dependent individuals, boundaries mean letting down their partners. They believe that by limiting the access the partners have to them, they are essentially locking them out, failing to love them unconditionally. Co-dependent individuals falsely believe that boundaries make their love conditional. They are afraid that if they don't acquiesce to their partner's wants, needs, and demands, their partner will find someone else.

- **Putting others' needs before their own:**
  Often, co-dependent individuals place their partner's needs above their own because they believe this is the ultimate expression of love. They believe that tending to their own needs makes them selfish when this is far from the truth. They never consider how their self-sacrificing ways can be detrimental to their wellbeing.

- **Fear of abandonment:**
  Because of their reliance on external validation, co-dependent individuals tend to fear abandonment. Their identity is greatly based on their ability to make the other person happy, which means that they will go to great lengths to keep the person from leaving them. For co-dependent individuals, even a hint of withdrawal is enough to drive them to desperation. They will do almost anything to make the other person notice them again, including giving in to absurd demands. Even if the relationship is not working, they still believe a hard time is worth it just as long as their partner doesn't leave them.

- **Poor self-esteem:**
  Individuals with poor self-esteem fail to recognize their own strengths because their focus is on what is "wrong" with them.

They have become accustomed to seeing their failures, shortcomings, and weaknesses that even when they accomplish anything great, they think it is a fluke. Because of this, they never believe they have done something good until someone else tells them. They become reliant on external validation. When their partner chooses them, this becomes one of the greatest validations they experience. Out of all the people they deem better, their partner chose them.

However, their low self-esteem doesn't magically change. Instead, the validation of being chosen only lasts a short while before they start worrying about being abandoned. Their self-talk is still critical, and to experience the high of validation again, they bend backwards for their partner. Their sense of worth becomes tied to their partner's validation, and they always seek ways of attaining it, even if it means ignoring their own needs.

> **Enabling behaviors:**

Enablers derive their sense of worth from anticipating the needs of others. While they may realize that the other person has a problem, they cannot bear being the "bad person," so they will always run to meet the other person's needs. They feel good when their partner relies on them, and they always look for ways to feel this validation. They believe that as long as their partner is happy, they are doing the right thing. Enablers feel important when they are rescuing and fixing others, even when it is clear to others that the situation is hopeless. They hold out hope that they will be the ones to save their partner, even though they are relying on their partner's shortcomings to boost their sense of self.

> **Difficulty expressing emotions:**
Co-dependent individuals go to great lengths to avoid confrontation or to make their partners angry. They believe that a peaceful façade is a sign of a happy relationship even though they may be harboring resentment for their partner. They choose to suffer in silence rather than expressing their own emotions or genuine thoughts. They may vent to friends and family, but they will always bite their tongue when it comes to their partner because they are afraid of losing their partner.

> **Loss of identity:**
Co-dependent individuals may become so immersed in their relationship that it becomes their identity. Their relationship becomes their greatest achievement, and they make decisions solely based on how the relationship is. When the relationship hits a rough patch, they feel personally responsible, and their esteems suffers. When the relationship is doing well, they are confident, happy, and upbeat. In this way, they lose sight of who they are, forgetting that they are independent beings in a relationship.

> **Feeling responsible for their partner's emotions:**
Co-dependent individuals feel responsible for their partner's emotions, especially the negative emotions. They take their partner's actions personally, even when it has nothing to do with them. When their partner is angry, they believe they must have done something to cause it. They overestimate their own influence over their partner, believing that everything they do influences their partner in some way. Because of this, they choose docility, believing that if they just go along with their partner, things will be grand. However, this doesn't make things

better. Their actions become deeply reliant on their partner's emotions and perceived reactions.

> **Jealousy and possessiveness:**
Because their partner represents a huge part of who they are, co-dependent individuals are highly possessive. They see threats even when they are none, and they are jealous of anyone else who gets their partner's attention. Co-dependent individuals find it difficult to see their partners as individuals with separate interests, and always seem to be calling or texting their partner when they are apart. They want their partner to look to them for all their needs and can't stand it when they see others fulfilling their partner's needs, no matter how mundane.

> **Difficulty ending unhealthy relationships:**
Co-dependent individuals have their entire identities wrapped up in their relationships. Losing a relationship, therefore, is akin to losing their entire identities. They have no idea who they are outside the relationship, which makes them unwilling to leave relationships that are clearly not working. They hold on tightly to their partners, suffering through disrespect, abuse, and resentment. They do not believe they can be happy without their partner, and they fail to see that they are suffering in the relationship. Even when their partner eventually leaves them, they spend a lot of time trying to get them back, which may cause them to settle in the role of the third party in their former partner's new relationship.

I know you love your partner and that means you want to do things for them, but how many things do they do for you? Is it an equal deal? If not, it's time to start assessing the situation honestly.

In fact, let's do that now.

EXERCISE 3: What Would You Do?

Look at these scenarios and identify which one you are most likely to do. Remember – be honest!

1. Your partner frequently cancels plans with you at the last minute. What do you do?

a) Get upset and feel rejected, but don't say anything to your partner
b) Try to understand why your partner canceled and offer to reschedule
c) Immediately assume that your partner is upset with you and apologize for something you may have done wrong

2. Your partner is struggling with addiction and frequently asks you to cover for them. What do you do?

a) Agree to cover for them, even if it means lying to others
b) Refuse to cover for them, but feel guilty and worried about their well-being
c) Offer to help them find treatment or support, but refuse to enable their addiction

3. Your partner frequently criticizes your appearance or behavior. What do you do?

a) Believe that your partner is right and try to change to meet their expectations
b) Get defensive and argue with your partner about their criticisms
c) Recognize that your partner's criticisms are not helpful or constructive, and set boundaries regarding what you are willing to tolerate

4. Your partner frequently asks you to sacrifice your own needs or desires for their benefit. What do you do?

a) Agree to sacrifice your own needs, even if it means neglecting your well-being
b) Try to find a compromise that meets both of your needs
c) Assert your own needs and desires, even if it means disappointing your partner

5. Your partner frequently becomes upset or angry when you spend time with friends or family. What do you do?

a) Cancel your plans with friends or family to avoid conflict with your partner
b) Try to reassure your partner that your relationship is important, but also maintain your own social connections
c) Feel guilty and anxious about spending time away from your partner, and avoid socializing altogether

Can you see which traits show up as co-dependency? Jumping to conclusions, feeling rejected without reason, and putting your own needs at the bottom of the priority list are all significant threats to a healthy relationship.

Answers:

1. *Co-dependent answer – C*
   Healthy answer - B

2. *Co-dependent answer – A*
   Healthy answer - C

3. *Co-dependent answer – A*
   Healthy answer - C

4. *Co-dependent answer – A*
   Healthy answer - B

5. *Co-dependent answer - A & C!*
   Healthy answer - B

> "There are only two states of being in the world of co-dependency – recovery and denial."
> – WENDY KAMINER

The Role of Negative Thoughts in Co-dependency

Negative thoughts can foster codependent behavior in several ways:

> **Low self-esteem:** It is impossible to have high self-esteem when your mind is constantly pointing out your flaws, failures, and weaknesses. When your internal dialog is mostly self-criticism, your reality will match your thoughts. So, when you find someone to validate your positive traits, it becomes easier to latch on to the person, hoping for the fleeting happiness that comes with validation. You begin doing everything to please the other person, hoping for a kind word, praise, or a reward for your good behavior. This reliance on the other person keeps growing, keeping you reliant on the whims of the other person.

> **Fear of rejection:** Negative thoughts drown out any positive emotions you have towards yourself. They convince you that you are not worthy of anything great, including companionship. You wonder how your friends can put up with you, and when you get into a relationship, you cannot stop wondering what your partner sees in you. These thoughts always tend to snowball, and you begin taking people's responses personally. You feel happy when someone agrees with you or accepts you, and you take any negative response personally.

> Even a simple "no" to a request becomes the big bad wolf in your world, and you can't stand people saying no since it gives the

negative thoughts even more power. To avoid what you perceive as rejection, you stop asking or making requests, choosing instead to focus on fulfilling the other person's wishes so they stay by your side.

- **Negative thoughts about your desirability:** Negative thoughts make it difficult for you to trust your ability to attract and keep a partner. Your focus is always on the ways you mess up, and you spend time worrying that your partner will finally realize that they made a mistake. You constantly seek their approval, looking for validation that they still like you. Even when your relationship turns sour, your thoughts convince you that you are not attractive enough to find someone else. Your partner is already putting up with you, and you feel the need to stay with them because you don't believe you have any other choice.

- **Difficulty expressing emotions:** When your thoughts are predominantly, you begin expecting the worst from any interaction. This means that even when you someone wrongs you, you imagine that speaking up will lead to a blow-out argument. You fear destroying the carefully constructed peace. The more you sit with your thoughts, the more convinced you become that you are in the wrong. You start believing that you are too sensitive, and that the situation isn't as bad as you're making it out to be.

- Even positive emotions are not spared. When something good happens, you fear that speaking about it will jinx it. You are always waiting for the other shoe to drop, and your brain becomes hyper vigilant. Negative thoughts curtail your emotional expression because you are convinced that expressing your emotions will have undesirable consequences.

It is important to address negative thoughts and work on developing a healthy sense of self-worth and self-esteem to avoid codependent behavior patterns.

You can learn to acknowledge when you're having a negative thought by asking yourself: "Is this thought useful, or is it negative?" If it's negative, it's time to reframe.

EXERCISE 4: Challenging Negative Thoughts

Reframing a negative thought means taking it, turning it on its head, and creating something positive out of it, and then repeating it until your brain accepts it as the truth.

It takes a while to achieve, but it's very effective; and over time, you'll notice that you become a more positive person.

Here is a step-by-step exercise to help you reframe negative thoughts. First, think of a negative thought you've had several times lately. Write it down here.

....
....
....
....
....
....
....
....

Now, follow these steps:

1. **Challenge the negative thought**: Once you have identified the negative thought, challenge it by asking yourself if it is true. For example, if your negative thought is "I'm not good enough," ask yourself if there is any evidence to support that thought. Is it really true that you are not good enough? Are there any examples that contradict that thought?

2. **Reframe the negative thought**: Once you have challenged the negative thought, reframe it into a positive thought. For example, if your negative thought is "I'm not good enough," reframe it into a positive thought such as "I am capable and worthy of success." Write it down below:

....
....
....
....
....
....
....
....
....

3. **Repeat the positive thought**: Repeat the positive thought to yourself several times, either out loud or in your head. This can help reinforce the positive thought and make it more believable.

4. **Practice:** Practice reframing negative thoughts into positive ones on a regular basis. The more you practice, the easier it will be to identify negative thoughts and reframe them.

Remember that reframing negative thoughts takes time and practice. Be patient with yourself and celebrate small successes along the way.

Let's Break it Down

The key takeaway from this chapter is that co-dependency needs to be addressed. It's particularly damaging in relationships because we pour so much of ourselves into them.

Now, if you have a good, supportive partner, they'll tell you that you need to take some time for yourself, and they'll do things for you in return. However, if you have a partner who doesn't recognize that you're doing far more for them than they are for you, the cycle will continue.

Of course, it might also be that you have a partner who enjoys being the center of attention, so they enable your co-dependency because it doesn't make any sense for them to get you to stop. Hopefully that's not the case for you, but unfortunately, it happens.

And I get it. Honestly, I do. You want people to like you, you want your partner to be happy in the relationship, and you're a kind person who just wants others to be content. But what about you? Don't you deserve to be happy and content?

Relying upon other people to make you happy is a mistake. The only person who can make you happy is yourself.

EXERCISE 5: Spot The Good Vs Bad Relationship

In our next chapter, we're going to talk about co-dependent vs interdependent relationships, but before we get there, let's see what you consider a healthy and unhealthy relationship. Place the words below in the column you feel fits best.

Jealousy	Possessiveness	Attention	Humor
Honesty	Trust	Support	Respect
Selfishness	Selflessness	Excitement	Spontaneity
Passion Fun	Fear	Empathy	

Healthy Relationship	Unhealthy Relationship

Now, take a clear look and ask yourself whether you've placed these words in the right column. Have a real, honest talk to yourself and brainstorm on each one. Can you recognize your relationship in either column?

"A healthy relationship will never require you to sacrifice your friends, your dreams, or your dignity."

– DINKAR KALOTRA

Chapter 2

Co-dependent vs Interdependent Relationships

Do you know what a healthy relationship looks like? It might sound like an odd question, but can you name the key traits that make up a healthy and supportive union?

I'm asking this question because if you're someone who is happy in a co-dependent relationship, you're obviously mistaken and perhaps it's because you simply don't know what it means to be in a healthy relationship.

Well, this chapter is going to shed some serious light on that.

> **EXERCISE 6: Are You Emotionally Dependent?**

How much do you rely upon your partner? Of course, it's normal to rely on them to a certain degree, but overreliance can be extremely damaging. Take this quiz to find out just how emotionally dependent you are on your partner.

1. Do you feel anxious or upset when you're not in contact with a particular person?

Yes/No

2. Do you rely on a specific person to provide you with emotional support or validation?

Yes/No

3. Do you feel like you need to be in constant communication with a particular person?

Yes/No

4. Have you ever neglected your own needs or responsibilities because of your relationship with a specific person?

Yes/No

5. Do you feel like you can't be happy or fulfilled without a particular person in your life?

Yes/No

6. Have you ever changed your behavior or personality to please a specific person?

Yes/No

7. Do you feel like you're constantly seeking approval or validation from a specific person?

Yes/No

8. Have you ever put your own safety or well-being at risk for the sake of a particular person?

Yes/No

9. Do you feel like you're unable to make decisions or act without consulting a specific person?

Yes/No

10. Do you feel like you're unable to cope with difficult emotions without the support of a specific person?

Yes/No

If you answered "yes" to several of these questions, it may be worth exploring the possibility that you have an unhealthy emotional dependency on a particular person. It's important to remember that it's okay to seek support from others, but it's important to have a healthy balance of self-reliance and support from others.

What About Your Relationship?

Before we go on, I want you to quickly scribble down any nagging concerns or doubts you have about your relationship. Don't think too much; just write down the first thing that come to your mind. I'll tell you why in a moment. And don't worry; nobody else is going to see this.

....

....

....

....

....

The reason I wanted you to do this is because in order to recognize that your relationship may be a little more one-sided than it should be, you must see it in black and white, written on paper. And when we compare co-dependent relationships to interdependent ones (the good type), perhaps that will help you to initiate change.

Let's compare them.

Co-dependent vs Interdependent Relationships

A co-dependent relationship is unbalanced. An interdependent relationship is more balanced, with focus on your partner, yourself, your friends, and family members. It's a hell of a lot healthier, that's for sure.

Co-dependent relationships and interdependent relationships are two different types of relationships. Here are some differences:

- **Focus on self vs. focus on others:** In a codependent relationship, the focus is primarily on the needs and desires of the other person. In an interdependent relationship, both partners are able to focus on their own needs and desires while also considering the needs and desires of the other person.
- **Boundaries:** In a codependent relationship, there may be a lack of boundaries between the two partners, with one person taking responsibility for the other person's emotions and actions. In an interdependent relationship, both partners are able to set and maintain healthy boundaries, respecting each other's individuality and autonomy.
- **Communication:** In a codependent relationship, communication may be limited or unhealthy, with one person avoiding conflict or confrontation in order to maintain the relationship. In an interdependent relationship, both

partners are able to communicate openly and honestly, even about difficult or uncomfortable topics.
- **Sense of self:** In a codependent relationship, one or both partners may have a diminished sense of self, with their identity and self-worth tied to the relationship. In an interdependent relationship, both partners are able to maintain a strong sense of self, with their identity and self-worth separate from the relationship.
- **Mutual support:** In a codependent relationship, one person may be overly reliant on the other person for emotional or practical support. In an interdependent relationship, both partners are able to provide mutual support and care for each other while also maintaining their own independence.

From that comparison, it's pretty clear that an interdependent relationship is what you should be aiming for.

> " Your relationships can only be as healthy as you are."
>
> – NEIL CLARK WARREN

EXERCISE 7: What Do You Want?

So, now you know that, scribble down what you want in a relationship. Be honest. If your relationship right now isn't serving you well, there is a chance to turn it around, but you need to know what you want before you initiate a conversation and action.

EXERCISE 8: Co-dependent or Interdependent?

Let's test how much of the last section has sunk into your mind, and whether your own relationship is happily interdependent or veering toward co-dependent. Remember to answer each question as honestly as you can. Nobody is judging you!

1. When making decisions, do you and your partner tend to:

    a) Always agree on what to do, even if it means sacrificing your own needs

    b) Compromise and find a solution that meets both your needs

    c) Sometimes disagree, but are able to communicate openly and find a solution that works for both of you

2. When you spend time with friends or family, does your partner:

    a) Get upset or angry, and try to prevent you from spending time away from them

    b) Encourage you to spend time with others, but also express their desire to spend time with you

    c) Support your social connections and encourage you to maintain your own interests and relationships

3. When you have a disagreement or conflict with your partner, do you tend to:

    a) Avoid confrontation and conflict, even if it means sacrificing your own needs or desires

    b) Express your own needs and desires, but also try to understand your partner's perspective

    c) Communicate openly and honestly, even about difficult or uncomfortable topics

4. When you are feeling stressed or overwhelmed, does your partner:

a) Try to fix or solve the problem for you, even if it means neglecting their own needs
b) Listen and offer support, but also encourage you to take care of yourself
c) Support you in finding healthy coping mechanisms and taking care of your own needs

5. When you think about your relationship, do you feel:

a) Like your identity and self-worth are tied to the relationship, and that you cannot be happy without it
b) Like you have a strong sense of self and identity, while also feeling connected and supported by your partner
c) Like you have a sense of independence and autonomy, but also feel overly reliant on your partner for emotional or practical support

Scoring: Give yourself one point for each "a" answer, two points for each "b" answer, and three points for each "c" answer.

- **5-7 points:** Your relationship may be co-dependent, and you may benefit from seeking professional help to address these patterns of behavior.

- **8-10 points:** Your relationship may have some co-dependent tendencies, and you could benefit from focusing on setting and maintaining healthy boundaries.

- **11-15 points:** Your relationship is likely interdependent, with a healthy balance of independence and interdependence. Congratulations on maintaining a healthy relationship!

Answers:

1. Co-dependent answer - A
   Interdependent answer - B

2. Co-dependent answer - A
   Interdependent answer – C (but B is good too!)

3. Co-dependent answer - A
   Interdependent answer – B & C

4. Co-dependent answer - A
   Interdependent answer - C

5. Co-dependent answer - A
   Interdependent answer - B

Are You Being Enabled?

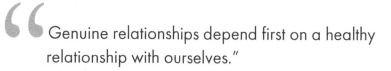

" Genuine relationships depend first on a healthy relationship with ourselves."

— SONIA CHOQUETTE

Sometimes a partner feeds a co-dependent person's behaviors because it suits them. It's not pleasant, and it's certainly not something you want to think about your own partner, but the truth is, we're all human. If someone is giving us everything, we might not want that to stop.

But if your partner loves you, they'll want what is best for you.

Before you address it, you need to know how to spot an enabler in a relationship.

It can be difficult to tell if your partner doesn't want you to stop being codependent, as they may not be aware of their own enabling behaviors or the impact that co-dependency is having on the relationship. However, here are some signs that your partner may not want you to stop being codependent:

> **They become upset or angry when you try to set boundaries:** Boundaries are essential in any relationship. Boundaries protect you, keeping you safe from bad actors. Healthy boundaries keep both parties independent and minimize the chances of one person exploiting the other.
>
> When your partner gets angry when you instill boundaries, this is not a good sign. If they are still angry after you explain how the boundaries are supposed to help, then they might be scared they cannot access you like they used to. At this stage, you need to reflect on how much access they had, and why they are fighting this. Co-dependent partners relate from a position of fear, and boundaries tend to feel like rejection.

> **They discourage you from seeking help:** When the status quo favors one person, they may not be willing to embrace any change. In fact, many will fight to keep things as they are. The same applies to a partner who's used to the dynamics of co-dependency, especially if they are the ones who gain more. Expressing the desire to seek help is a threat to the relationship dynamics, something your partner may not be keen on.
>
> They may not directly discourage you from seeking help, and they may instead keep reminding you of why it is not a viable idea. They may remind you of your previous failed attempts, highlight the cost, or how you may not have enough time to undertake this new plan. The discouragement may be more

subtle, like asking for things to be done when you're supposed to be leaving the house, expressing their desire to spend time with you when you're supposed to have an appointment, or becoming more attentive so that you conclude that there's nothing wrong with the relationship.

> **They rely on you for emotional or practical support:** Does your partner have a support system that doesn't include you? Do they have someone they can reach out to or are you the only one they call on for help? When someone relied on us, we feel great about ourselves. We feel like we matter. However, there should a limit to how much someone relies on another. If you are the only one your partner leans on, this is a sign that they are overly reliant on you, which is not good for them. The validation of being someone's savior is not worth the risk to their wellbeing. Your partner's ability to maintain relationships with others is important for a healthy relationship.

So, if you notice that your partner basically relies on you for everything, reevaluate the dynamics of your relationship.

> **They guilt-trip you when you try to express your needs:** How does your partner respond when you honestly express your desires and needs? This is usually evident when your request casts into light that one party is getting more out of the other. To protect the dynamics of the relationship and keep you dependent on them, your partner may listen to what you say and promise to do better. However, they will slowly start to make you feel guilty for asking by highlighting how your request is now inconveniencing them.

If you asked for their help with chores, they may grumble about how cleaning up is affecting their back; how the chores are robbing them of time to rest and impacting their work; or how they now have little time to focus on you. They may not be direct in their approach, and instead they may complain loudly even as they work. Weaponized incompetence is also another way they will enforce the status quo. By performing the actions badly and highlighting just how bad they are, you will feel sorry for them and take up the work again.

This happens even for non-physical requests. The bottom line is that they need you dependent, and they will sabotage any attempt to become more assertive, sometimes unknowingly.

> **They refuse to acknowledge the impact of co-dependency on the relationship:** When one party is benefiting from the dynamics of the relationship, they will never admit that things are as bad as they really are. As you express the idea that your relationship may not healthy as it's supposed to be, they will not see it the same way. They may not even be aware that they are doing it. They will make excuses for any situations they highlight, or they will show you why your thinking is wrong. They will reframe events in ways that make them seem inconsequential.

In some cases, they will even deny the occurrence of said event. This can be done by any of the parties, not necessarily the one who is benefiting from the co-dependence. This is usually the most difficult situation to deal with, since they are convinced they are right. And changing someone's account of events is difficult because they tend to trust their own recollections. "Things can't be that bad," they'll maintain. Breaking free from this requires the participation of both parties, and ability for both of you to recognize the signs and consequences of co-dependence.

Now, before you start accusing your partner of all sorts of things, remember that they may not even know that they're enabling your co-dependence. It may be that they've simply fallen into a routine, and it's become 'the way things are'. By shaking things up a little, you can bring fresh energy into your relationship. But the best answer? An open, honest, conversation.

EXERCISE 9: Spot the Enabler

Co-dependency can be a very positive thing for the receiving partner, but a pretty negative thing for you. It can be very tough to spot, but it's important if you want to right the balance in your union.

Take this quiz to sharpen your enabler-spotting skills.

Scenario 1 – You always make dinner for your partner, but this particular day you're not feeling so well. You suggest your partner makes dinner, what do they do?

    a) They suggest ordering in.
    b) They tell you that your cooking is much better than theirs, so you give in.
    c) They make dinner themselves.

Which option spots the enabler? – B. Enablers often use guilt as a tactic to get you to give them what they're used to getting.

Scenario 2 – A close friend has invited you out to dinner and drinks to celebrate her promotion. There will be several other women there. What does your partner say?

    a) They don't want you to go. Instead, they suggest you spend the night together.
    b) They encourage you to go and have fun.

c) They're not thrilled, but you go anyway. They call you several times during the evening, and in the end, you go home early.

Which option spots the enabler? – A. Although C isn't great either. But option A shows that your partner just wants you there to wait on them hand and foot. They also don't want you to have fun without them.

Scenario 3 – You're feeling a little low because you're having problems at work. You try to tell your partner about what's going on. What do they do?

a) They listen to you and give advice.
b) They pretend to listen but in reality, they're playing on their cellphone.
c) They tell you that you're probably imagining it.

Which option spots the enabler? – B. While C might seem like enabler-behavior, it's actually far more toxic than that! B is more likely to be enabler-style; they'll pretend they're doing something for you, but they're really not.

Are You Doing the Enabling?

It could very well be that your partner has co-dependent traits to a certain degree too. It's definitely worth thinking about! And because you're co-dependent, it makes sense for you to keep them that way, so you can maintain control in the relationship and not feel like you're out of control.

Take this quiz to find out if you're guilty of enabling behavior.

EXERCISE 10: Are You an Enabler?

I know you might not like the idea of being an enabler, but it's important to explore all areas if you want to break free of any type of co-dependency in your life. Take this quiz to find out the truth.

When someone you care about is struggling with a problem, how do you typically respond?

- a) I offer support and encouragement, but ultimately let them handle it on their own
- b) I take charge and try to solve the problem for them
- c) I avoid the problem and hope it goes away on its own
- d) I feel overwhelmed and unsure of what to do

Do you often make excuses for someone's bad behavior?

- a) No, I hold them accountable for their actions
- b) Yes, I try to justify their behavior to others or to myself
- c) Sometimes, depending on the situation
- d) I don't know

Do you find yourself constantly trying to please others, even if it means sacrificing your own needs?

- a) No, I prioritize my needs and boundaries
- b) Yes, I feel like I have to put others first in order to be liked or accepted
- c) Sometimes, depending on the situation
- d) I don't know

Have you ever lied or covered up for someone's addiction or unhealthy behavior?

- a) No, I believe in honesty and transparency
- b) Yes, I feel like I have to protect them from consequences or judgment

c) Sometimes, depending on the situation
d) I don't know

Do you feel responsible for someone else's happiness or well-being?

a) No, I believe that everyone is responsible for their own happiness and well-being
b) Yes, I feel like it's my job to make sure they're happy and taken care of
c) Sometimes, depending on the situation
d) I don't know

If you answered mostly (b) or (c) to these questions, it may be worth exploring the possibility that you are enabling others and contributing to co-dependent dynamics in your relationships.

It's important to remember that enabling behaviors can be harmful to both you and the person you're trying to help.

How to Change Your Relationship

Now you're more aware of what enabling behavior looks like, let's remember one important thing:

Enabling behavior can sometimes be unconscious or unintentional. Enablers may believe that they are helping the person they are enabling, or they may feel guilty or responsible for the person's problems and believe that they need to rescue or protect them. It can be difficult for enablers to recognize their enabling behavior, but it is important for them to do so in order to break the cycle and help the person they are enabling to take responsibility for their own actions and make positive changes in their life.

So, it may not be that your partner is consciously enabling your behavior at all. However, the issue really lies with you. If you can stop being co-dependent, your partner will have no choice but to accept it. But again, an honest conversation is necessary, and here are a few tips to help you with that:

> **Be honest and direct** - Let your partner know that you have recognized your co-dependence and that you want to make changes to improve your relationship and your life.

> **Explain your reasons** - Share your reasons for wanting to be less co-dependent, such as wanting to have a healthier relationship, wanting to be more independent, or wanting to take care of your own needs.

> **Share your plan** - Let your partner know what steps you plan to take to be less co-dependent, such as setting boundaries, seeking therapy, or practicing self-care.

> **Ask for support** - Ask your partner for their support and understanding as you work to make changes in your behavior. Let them know that this is not about blaming them, but about taking responsibility for your own actions and improving your relationship.

> **Be open to feedback** - Be open to hearing your partner's thoughts and feelings about your co-dependent behavior and be willing to listen and make changes.

Remember, change takes time and effort, so be patient with yourself and your partner as you work towards a healthier, more balanced relationship.

You can do it!

"How you love yourself is how you teach others to love you."

— RUPI KAUR

Chapter 3

Who Are You?

When you're naturally co-dependent, or you've developed those habits over time, it's very easy to lose sight of yourself. Of course, you recognize your reflection in the mirror, but the inner you? You're not too sure who that is anymore.

The tricky thing here is that you won't realize it. It will sneak upon you and steal your true identity, and you won't know anything about it until it clicks one day that you can't recall who you are anymore.

It's because you've put your own needs and wants aside for so long that you've basically become subservient to everyone else in your life. But your needs and wants should matter just as much as theirs – seriously, it's time to make that a mantra!

Repeat after me: I matter! My needs and wants matter!

Say it loud and say it proud!

For a moment, I want you to think about all the things you used to love but no longer do anymore. And then, ask yourself why. Is it because you outgrew them? Did your tastes change? Or is it because you put them aside for something else?

Write down a few thoughts here:

....
....
....
....
....
....
....
....
....
....
....
....
....
....
....
....
....
....
....
....

Writing that list might have made you remember things you forgot, and you might have a desire to do them again. Don't push it aside! Make a plan to incorporate those things into your life and make spending time on them a priority.

It's easy to think that spending time on hobbies is just spare time and not really important, but it is. It's about indulging in the things you like; it's self-care. Otherwise, life is all work, and where's the fun in that?

Why Maintaining Your Sense of Self in a Relationship is Important

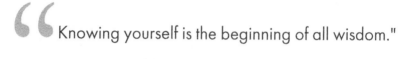
" Knowing yourself is the beginning of all wisdom."

— ARISTOTLE

Retaining your identity in a relationship is important because it helps you maintain your sense of self and individuality. It is common for people in a relationship to start adopting their partner's interests, hobbies, and even personality traits. While it is natural to have some common interests and to influence each other, it is important to maintain your own identity and not lose yourself completely in the relationship.

Here are some reasons why retaining your identity in a relationship is important:

> **It helps you maintain your self-esteem and confidence:** Staking your entire life on your relationship is not healthy because it means that the events of the relationship will directly impact how you see yourself. However, separating your identity from your relationship allows you to see things more objectively. You can understand that what happens in your relationship does not dictate who you are. Rather, it only gives you insight into your weaknesses and strengths when relating to a partner.

Any challenges within the relationship are dealt with as challenges, not threats to your identity. This ability to step back and see things clearly affirms your self-esteem and boosts your confidence.

> **It helps you maintain your independence:** A level of independence within a relationship is vital in keeping the relationship healthy. When both parties are independent individuals with interests, hobbies, and stability even when they are apart, the relationship becomes a partnership where they both choose to be together. This is not the case if one party is reliant on the other.

This independence means that even when your partner is not available, you can still have a good time. You are not frustrated or blowing up their phone. Rather, you understand that time apart doesn't mean that there's something wrong with the relationship. It is just time spent on things they love, which will make them happy.

> **It helps you maintain your friendships and social connections:** Losing yourself in a relationship always seems inevitable for some people, but this is not healthy. A romantic partnership is supposed to complement your other relationships, not replace them. Having a support system outside your partner is great for your wellbeing, and this should always be encouraged in relationships. Your identity is a culmination of who you are in and out of the relationship, and keeping your family and friends close should be a no-brainer.

> **It helps you maintain a healthy relationship:** Having the time and space to indulge in your own interests is a great way of taking care of yourself. Even when your partner is not around, you can still have a good time and spare yourself the frustration of

waiting idly for them to finish what they are doing. When both parties are free and open to engage in activities that bring them joy, they are more likely to seek out their partners out of pleasure, not because it is an obligation. Time apart is just as important as time together, and this makes the relationship a haven.

When co-dependence is a huge part of the relationship, time spent apart is likely to cause friction. Both parties then choose to remain within the vicinity of their partner just to avoid fighting, not because they genuinely desire to spend time with the other person. This creates resentment, and it may lead to one partner lashing out at the other. Time together should be pleasurable, not an obligation to suffer through.

EXERCISE 11: I Love Myself!

When you morph into someone else in a relationship, you forget how to love yourself. Every trait and quirk that makes you who you are is equally important as theirs, if not more so. If you don't love yourself, how can anyone else?

So, it's time fall in love with yourself all over again. Doing so will require some deep thinking; it might be that you've forgotten a lot about your real identity, but this exercise will get you thinking and open up the channels of self-love once again.

Try this:

1. Set aside some time every day for you. It only needs to be 20-30 minutes or so.
2. During that time, spend some time thinking about all the things you love about yourself.

3. Write down as many positive things about yourself as you can think of.
4. Take a moment to admire your list and feel the sense of positivity wash over you.
5. Every day from then, add 1-2 things to your list. Never go a day without adding something!
6. After two weeks, sit down and examine your list. Can you see how wonderful you are and why you don't need to change yourself for anyone?
7. Remember to look at this list regularly, to help keep your identity in place.

What is Your Trigger?

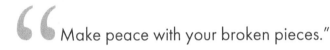
"Make peace with your broken pieces."

– R.H. SIN

Nobody is totally co-dependent all the time. It's very likely that there are certain triggers that push you toward this type of behavior. Once you understand those triggers, you can do something about them, e.g., minimize them, avoid them, or face them.

Facing your triggers might be scary, but it will help you overcome them for the rest of your days, and they won't be so scary anymore.

Everyone is different, and your trigger may be something totally different to anyone else's. However, there are a few common triggers of co-dependent behavior:

> **Perceived withdrawal:** Our reaction to certain situations may stem from prior experience, especially those we endured during

our formative years. If our parents or loved ones ignored us when we misbehaved, we become especially sensitive to our ability to hold our partner's attention. So, whenever we feel like they are closed off from us, we panic and try everything possible to get their attention and validation. This trigger does not even have to be real to put us in a tailspin. Our partner may be genuinely busy, but our past experience does not allow us to objectively analyze the situation. Instead, the panic takes hold and rush to make amends.

> **Need for control:** When we are co-dependent, our partners' independence feels like a threat to the relationship. We imagine that if they have other activities outside the relationship, they may walk away from us. To avoid this, we make sure to tie in our lives with theirs as much as possible to maintain the feeling of control. When the feeling of control is threatened, we react by trying to bring our partner back into the fold; by making sure that they rely solely on us again.

> **Fear of abandonment:** For many people in co-dependent relationship, their fear of abandonment runs deep. They are unable to let go of the relationship even if they are hurting because they would have to admit failure. They cannot seem to believe in their ability to find better relationships, so they remain rooted in the familiar. Even when the relationship turns violent, they find ways of justifying the violence and they still hold on.

The fear of abandonment trumps their own self-preservation.

> **Trauma:** Traumatic experiences, such as physical or emotional abuse, can create dependency as a coping mechanism. When we experience traumatic events, we seek safety anywhere we can. And sometimes we equate the familiar with safety. So, even

though the relationship is not working out, we remain rooted in it because we know the patterns and we understand how to deal with them. Trauma response is not always healthy, and it's not uncommon for traumatized individuals to depend on partners who are abusive and hold on to them just because the alternative is scarier.

It's important to recognize these triggers and work on developing healthy coping mechanisms and boundaries to break the cycle of co-dependency.

EXERCISE 12: Identifying Your Personal Triggers

If you sit down and think about your triggers, it's likely you won't be able to point them out. Triggers are buried deep in our subconscious minds, and it's hard to work out what pushes you to act in a certain way right off the bat. However, journaling can help you discover what pushes you toward negative behaviors.

You can use a journal for so many things, but working out behavioral patterns is one of the most useful benefits.

So, use the space below to jot down your thoughts and feelings. It might be useful to do it at the end of each day, so you have a full view of the day.

> - If you acted in a codependent way, write down what you did.
> - Write down how you felt before, during, and after the action.
> - Explore what happened before you felt pushed into acting in this way, which could have triggered your co-dependence.
> - Continue this process for 2 weeks to a month.

Who Are You?

> After time has passed, sit down, and look for patterns. Can you identify specific situations, emotions, or words that push you toward acting in a co-dependent way?

Once you identify a trigger, you have three choices.

- **Avoid it** – Actively avoid facing the trigger to avoid co-dependent behavior. This is a difficult one because you can't avoid all situations in life, nor should you have to!
- **Minimize it** – What can you do to minimize the impact this trigger has on you?
- **Face it** – Face it head on. Be brave and question it. Pull it apart until it no longer has any control over you.

And if you ask me, I think you should face it. Go on, be courageous and kick that trigger out of your life for good!

It's Time to Reclaim Your Power

> "To fall in love with yourself is the first secret to happiness."
> – ROBERT MORELY

Finding your identity again after experiencing co-dependency can be a challenging process, but it's an important step in developing healthy relationships and improving your overall well-being.

Here are some tips on how to find your identity again after co-dependency:

Practice self-care

Focusing on yourself after relying on someone else can be difficult, but it is doable. Self-care is more than just spa days and fine dining. Self-care, in this sense, involves doing things that make you feel good about yourself. Things that make you realize that you are strong and capable. Self-care is as simple as resting when you are tired, or getting yourself a treat when you accomplish something.

Self-care gives you a chance to be your own friend, to trust yourself again, and to believe in your capabilities. Self-care is as simple as eating healthier, choosing to exercise, and being kinder to yourself.

Explore your interests

What are the things that make you smile? What activity gives you pleasure? When you indulge in activities that make you happy or content, you learn how to enjoy even the most mundane activities. Embracing activities that keep you content show you how to embrace peace and joyful moments. When you know how it feels to be happy with yourself, you find it more difficult to stay in situations that make you sad.

As you get better at the activities you choose, you become more confident in your abilities. And depending on the activities, you may join a community of like-minded individuals, which gives your social life a positive boost.

Set boundaries

Boundaries are essential in any relationship, and setting healthy boundaries keeps you from further harm, either by staying in situations that don't work, or by allowing people access to you even after they cause you harm. Healthy boundaries are the hallmark of healthy relationships, and you must understand your needs before you embark on creating boundaries that work for you. We're going to explore this further in the next chapter.

Seek support

Support, from professionals or loved ones, is fundamental when you're trying to make significant changes in your life. And choosing to free yourself from co-dependence is a daunting task, especially if your triggers are rooted in childhood conditioning or trauma response. Co-dependence is your comfort zone, and trying to escape it may be harder than you think, even if you are ready to take the step. If you feel like you cannot make it out alone, or if you find yourself slipping into your old habits, seek support.

If your trigger is trauma or emotional responses, finding a therapist or behavioral psychologist to guide you through may be your best bet. Family and friends can keep you accountable, but you have to be careful not to transfer your dependency to others. Allow yourself to reach out to others, and if you can, join a support group. Sharing your experiences with people who understand your situation is empowering, and can be the motivation you need to face the challenges and push to grow stronger.

Practice self-reflection

Change cannot happen when we don't know the extent of the problem. Just like a doctor cannot treat a disease until they complete the diagnosis, you cannot embrace your individuality until you understand the cause and consequences of your co-dependency. What triggered the co-dependency? How did it impact your life?

To achieve this, you must take time and self-reflect. Whether this is done in the therapist's office or in the comfort of your home doesn't matter. What matters is that you have to be honest with yourself. You need to sit with the discomfort of your past actions to recognize the patterns of behavior and triggers that got you in the unfortunate situation in the first place. Self-reflection is difficult, painful, and outright exhausting, but it is an important part of rediscovering yourself. It is crucial if you are to reconnect with who you are, or to uncover your true self.

Self-reflection is you path to recovery, and you need to keep at it even when you think you are fine. To understand and embrace your true self, take the time to recognize that the good and the bad are just as important. This comprehension will fuel your desire for change, making it easier to commit to the changes you make.

Remember, finding your identity after co-dependency is a process that takes time and patience. Be kind to yourself and focus on taking small steps towards your goals each day. With time and effort, you can rediscover your sense of self and enjoy a relationship that enhances your life, not one that replaces your identity.

Do You Need Control?

Part of learning who you are again comes down to understanding the nitty-gritty, and some of those details may not be pleasant. But remember, we all have good and bad traits, and we can use the slightly negative points and learn from them.

One point that many people with co-dependent behaviors need to deal with is the desire for control. In the end, co-dependence is a form of control because you're doing things for others so they don't leave you. It may sound like a less negative type of control, but it's still damaging.

Overcoming the need to control comes down to self-esteem, but first you need to know whether this is a problem for you.

EXERCISE 13: Give Me Control!

Remember, it's normal to not like every small thing about yourself, but you have to acknowledge that you have good and bad points too – just like everyone! If you feel that you do need help letting go of the reins, that's fine. The first step is acknowledgement.

Answer these questions as honestly as you can.

Do you often feel anxious or uncomfortable when things don't go according to plan?

a) No, I'm usually able to adapt to changes in plans
b) Yes, I feel like I need to be in control of every situation
c) Sometimes, depending on the situation
d) I don't know

Do you feel like you need to be in charge of every decision in your relationships?

a) No, I believe in collaboration and compromise
b) Yes, I feel like I need to make all the decisions to ensure things go smoothly
c) Sometimes, depending on the situation
d) I don't know

Do you find yourself criticizing or correcting others frequently?

a) No, I believe in respecting others' choices and opinions
b) Yes, I feel like I need to point out others' mistakes or flaws in order to help them improve
c) Sometimes, depending on the situation
d) I don't know

Do you feel like you need to be involved in every aspect of your partner's life?

   a) No, I believe in giving my partner space and respecting their privacy
   b) Yes, I feel like I need to know everything about my partner's life in order to feel secure
   c) Sometimes, depending on the situation
   d) I don't know

Have you ever tried to change or control someone else's behavior or habits?

   a) No, I believe in accepting others for who they are
   b) Yes, I feel like I need to change others in order to feel comfortable or secure
   c) Sometimes, depending on the situation
   d) I don't know

If you answered mostly (b) or (c) to these questions, it may be worth exploring the possibility that you have a need for control and how it may be contributing to co-dependent tendencies. It's important to remember that trying to control others can be harmful to you and the person you're trying to control.

"Daring to set boundaries is about having the courage to love ourselves even when we risk disappointing others."

– BRENE BROWN

Chapter 4

Don't Cross My Boundaries

Lack of boundaries in a relationship can easily lead to one person doing far more than the other. One partner can easily feel taken advantage of or taken for granted if boundaries aren't in place.

Setting boundaries in a relationship means establishing clear guidelines and expectations for what is, and is not, acceptable behavior from your partner. It involves communicating your needs and limits and working with your partner to come to an agreement on how to maintain a healthy and respectful relationship.

Here are some examples of what setting boundaries in a relationship might look like:

> **Communicating your needs:** This might involve telling your partner what you need in order to feel respected and loved, such as spending quality time together, receiving compliments or affection, or having alone time.

> **Establishing limits:** This might involve setting limits on behavior that is not acceptable in the relationship, such as name-calling, yelling, or physical violence.

> **Negotiating compromises:** This might involve working with your partner to come to an agreement on how to handle certain situations, such as how to divide household chores or how to handle disagreements.

> **Respecting your partner's boundaries:** Setting boundaries is a two-way street, and it's important to respect your partner's boundaries as well. This might involve asking for permission before sharing personal information, respecting their need for alone time, or not pressuring them to do something they are uncomfortable with.

However, you can set a boundary on anything that is important to you. Hell, if you hate spaghetti and it makes you feel physically ill, you could have a boundary that your partner doesn't eat it around you! Boundaries are there to make you feel comfortable, and if spaghetti doesn't do that, well, it's gotta go!

Here are some reasons why setting boundaries is important:

> **Establishing mutual respect:** Setting boundaries helps establish mutual respect between partners. It communicates what is, and is not, acceptable behavior in the relationship and helps prevent any misunderstandings or conflicts that may arise.

> **Maintaining individuality:** Setting boundaries helps maintain individuality within the relationship. It allows each partner to have their own space, interests, and opinions, and prevents one partner from dominating or controlling the other.

> **Creating a healthy and balanced relationship:** Setting boundaries helps create a healthy and balanced relationship by ensuring that both partners are able to express their needs and feelings, and that both partners are willing to compromise and work together to maintain the relationship.

> **Preventing resentment and conflict:** When boundaries are not set, it can lead to resentment and conflict in the relationship. This can be avoided by setting clear and reasonable boundaries that both partners agree to.

> **Improving communication:** Setting boundaries requires open and honest communication between partners. This can help improve communication in the relationship, leading to a stronger and more fulfilling connection.

Setting boundaries can help you avoid or correct co-dependence, but the key is setting boundaries and sticking to them.

EXERCISE 14: Healthy Vs. Unhealthy Expectations

Below is a quiz with each question featuring a scenario. Choose whether you think this is a healthy or unhealthy boundary. Think carefully, as some might not be as clear as you might think!

1. Your partner checks in on you several times throughout the day. Is this a healthy or unhealthy boundary?
A. Healthy
B. Unhealthy

2. Your partner feels left out when you spend time with friends or family without them. Is this a healthy or unhealthy boundary?

A. Healthy
B. Unhealthy

3. Your partner often tells you what they think looks good on you, and you often follow their advice. Is this a healthy or unhealthy boundary?

A. Healthy
B. Unhealthy

4. Your partner asks if they can have your social media passwords and says that you can have theirs in return. Is this a healthy or unhealthy boundary?

A. Healthy
B. Unhealthy

5. Your partner often tells you quite firmly when you don't look good or you do something wrong. Is this a healthy or unhealthy boundary?

A. Healthy
B. Unhealthy

6. Your partner respects your need for alone time and encourages you to pursue your interests and hobbies. Is this a healthy or unhealthy boundary?

A. Healthy
B. Unhealthy

7. Your partner initially listens when you say you don't want sex but is quite persistent. Is this a healthy or unhealthy boundary?

A. Healthy
B. Unhealthy

8. Your partner respects your privacy and never touches your phone. Is this a healthy or unhealthy boundary?

A. Healthy
B. Unhealthy

Answers:

1. B - Unhealthy
2. B - Unhealthy
3. B - Unhealthy
4. B - Unhealthy
5. B - Unhealthy
6. A - Healthy
7. B - Unhealthy
8. A - Healthy

Explanation:

1. Checking in on your partner constantly can be a sign of controlling behavior and is an unhealthy boundary.
2. Your partner should respect your need for time with friends and family, and getting jealous or annoyed when you spend time without them is an unhealthy boundary.
3. Your partner should not be controlling your appearance and telling you how to dress, style your hair, or apply makeup. This is an unhealthy boundary.

4. Your partner should respect your privacy and not want access to your personal accounts. This is an unhealthy boundary.
5. Criticizing and putting down your partner is a sign of emotional abuse and is an unhealthy boundary, even if it doesn't initially come across as criticism.
6. Encouraging your partner to pursue their interests and hobbies and respecting their need for alone time is a sign of a healthy boundary.
7. Your partner should respect your boundaries and not pressure you into sex. This is an unhealthy boundary.
8. Respecting your partner's privacy and not going through their personal belongings without their permission is a sign of a healthy boundary.

What Do You Need in a Relationship?

" Walls keep everybody out. Boundaries teach people where the door is."

– UNKNOWN

Boundaries help you work out the things you need in a relationship and the things you don't. When you have these things, and you're free from the stuff you don't want, you'll find it much easier to be less co-dependent.

For instance, if your partner is naturally a flirty person, you're going to feel a little insecure. This could push you toward co-dependent behaviors. But if your boundary is that they don't flirt like this in your presence (or preferably at all), you won't feel the need to act in a negative way.

💡 EXERCISE 15: Let's Be Honest!

So, think carefully about some things you need in a relationship, and write them down here:

....
....
....
....
....
....
....

Now, write down the things that you don't want to have to deal with in a relationship.

....
....
....
....
....
....
....
....

EXERCISE 16: What Boundaries Do You Need to Set?

Telling you that you need to set boundaries and letting you think about it is all dandy, but you might not have a clue! In that case, a quiz might help. SO, here's a quiz to help you identify your personal boundaries and how well you are able to enforce them:

When someone asks me for a favor, I usually:

   a) Say yes, even if it inconveniences me
   b) Consider the request and decide whether or not it aligns with my values and priorities
   c) Say no, unless it is something I truly want to do

When someone makes a comment that offends me, I usually:

   a) Get upset and confrontational
   b) Ignore it and try to move on
   c) Address it politely but firmly

When someone tries to cross a boundary I have set, I usually:

   a) Get angry and defensive
   b) Let them cross it, even if it makes me uncomfortable
   c) Reassert my boundary in a calm and assertive manner

When someone tries to guilt-trip me into doing something, I usually:

   a) Get defensive and argumentative
   b) Give in and do what they want
   c) Acknowledge their feelings but assert my own needs and boundaries

When someone is being overly critical or demanding of me, I usually:

   a) Get defensive and shut down
   b) Take their criticism to heart and try to please them
   c) Consider their feedback but also assert my own needs and boundaries

When I need space or alone time, I usually:

   a) Withdraw without explanation or warning
   b) Feel guilty and try to push through it
   c) Communicate my needs clearly and respectfully

Scoring:

For each question, give yourself the following points:

A = 1 point
B = 2 points
C = 3 points

Add up your total score and see which category you fall into:

6-12 points: You may struggle with setting and enforcing personal boundaries. Consider seeking support or resources to help you develop this skill.

13-18 points: You have a strong ability to set and enforce personal boundaries. Keep up the good work and continue to prioritize your own needs and well-being.

Communicating Your Boundaries

Talking to your partner about relationship boundaries can be a sensitive topic, but it's important for establishing a healthy and respectful relationship. Here are some tips on how to have this conversation:

- ❯ **Take time to reflect:** Before you talk to your partner, take some time to reflect on what your boundaries are and why they are important to you. This will help you communicate your needs more clearly.

- ❯ **Choose the right time and place:** Choose a time and place where you and your partner can have a private conversation without distractions. Make sure you are both in a calm and receptive state of mind.

- ❯ **Use "I" statements:** When discussing boundaries, use "I" statements to express how you feel and what you need. This can help prevent your partner from feeling attacked or defensive.

- ❯ **Be specific:** Clearly communicate your boundaries and expectations. Use specific examples to help your partner understand what you mean.

- ❯ **Listen to your partner:** Allow your partner to express their own boundaries and needs. Listen actively and try to understand their perspective.

- ❯ **Be willing to compromise:** Establishing boundaries is a two-way street. Be willing to compromise and find a solution that works for both of you.

> **Follow through:** Once you've established your boundaries, follow through on them. If your partner crosses a boundary, gently remind them of your agreement and work together to find a solution.

Have you ever wondered what your communication style is? That can tell you a lot about how you face problems or perhaps run from them. Let's do a quiz to find out yours.

EXERCISE 17: What is Your Communication Style?

Answer each question honestly!

1. When someone asks for my opinion, I usually:

    a) Tell them what I think they want to hear
    b) Consider my own thoughts and feelings, but also take their perspective into account
    c) Speak my mind without much consideration for their feelings or needs

2. When someone is upset with me, I usually:

    a) Apologize and try to make things right, even if I don't think I did anything wrong
    b) Listen to their perspective and try to find a solution that works for both of us
    c) Get defensive and argumentative

3. When I'm feeling overwhelmed or stressed, I usually:

    a) Keep it to myself and try to push through it
    b) Reach out to a trusted friend or family member for support
    c) Expect others to anticipate my needs and take care of me

4. When someone disagrees with me, I usually:

a) Back down and avoid conflict
b) Respect their opinion but also assert my own perspective
c) Get upset and defensive

5. When I need help or support, I usually:

a) Feel guilty and ashamed for asking
b) Ask for help in a clear and direct manner
c) Expect others to anticipate my needs and offer help without me having to ask

6. When I'm in a conflict with someone, I usually:

a) Avoid confrontation and try to keep the peace
b) Listen to their perspective and try to find a solution that works for both of us
c) Get angry and confrontational

Scoring:

For each question, give yourself the following points:

A = 1 point
B = 2 points
C = 3 points

Add up your total score and see which category you fall into:

6-9 points: You may struggle with assertive communication and may tend to be passive or passive-aggressive. Consider seeking support or resources to help you develop assertiveness skills.

10-12 points: You have a moderate ability to communicate assertively, but may benefit from further practice and support.

13-18 points: You have a strong ability to communicate assertively and effectively. Keep up the good work and continue to prioritize clear and respectful communication in your relationships.

Remember, If your partner loves you, which I hope they do, then there should be no issue in this boundary-setting conversation. It could be that they simply don't realize you're not happy or that you're not getting what you need. This conversation should clear that up.

However, if the opposite is true, it's time to ask yourself whether you really need this type of relationship. I know it's hard, but toxic relationships will only drag you further down. You really don't need it, and you certainly deserve better.

EXERCISE 18: Spot The Boundary

I know it can be hard to work out exactly what a boundary should be for a specific situation. For instance, you might know that your partner going out with their friends and not texting you once throughout the evening makes you suspicious and sad. But you must remember that boundaries work both ways; you can't tell them that they can't go! So, what can you say instead?

In this case, you could ask your partner to message you at least once while they're out, just so you know they're okay. From there, you have to deal with your suspicious mind and trust them.

Let's look at some scenarios and work out suitable boundaries for each.

Scenario 1: Your partner comes home from work, and they spend most of the evening scrolling through social media or texting their friends. This makes you feel neglected and a little jealous.

What boundary could be set here?

1. Ask your partner not to use their phone when they're at home, as you've missed them all day.
2. Ask your partner to limit their social media use and not to speak to friends all night long – ask that you have 'couple time.'
3. Don't do anything; they're allowed to speak to other people.

Best boundary option: Option 2. You can't tell your partner they can't talk to their friends or check their social media; this is what co-dependent people do! However, they should respect you enough not to remain glued to their phone the entire night. This boundary gives everyone the best of both worlds.

Scenario 2: Your partner is still very good friends with their ex. You know there is nothing going on, but you don't like it when they go out for coffee or speak to each other via text.

What boundary could be set here?

1. Ban your partner from speaking to their ex.
2. Ask that your partner involves you too, i.e., that you can go along the next time they meet.
3. Suck it up; you know they're not together and you should get over yourself.

Best boundary option: Option 2. If they're good friends, there's not a lot you can do about it. Banning your partner from seeing them will only make them resentful and feel that they're not trusted. However, that doesn't mean you should put up with something that makes you feel so bad either. Option 2 means that you get to be friends with their ex too, and that way, you can see there's nothing to be fearful of.

Scenario 3: When your partner has been out with their friends, they often come home drunk, loud, and easily triggered into anger. They never hurt you, but you don't like the way they behave.

What boundary could be set here?

1. Ask your partner to stay with a friend if they've had too much to drink.
2. Ask them not to go out with their friends during the evenings anymore.
3. Ask your partner to be more mindful of how much they're drinking and how they behave when they're home. Explain that next time, you will simply remain silent and go to bed.

Best boundary option: Option 3. You won't be happy if they stay out all night, and you can't ban them from going out with their friends either. So, option 3 works well here. Asking them to be more mindful of what they're doing isn't too much to ask, and by saying that you will simply walk away without a reaction, you're protecting your own wellbeing. However, you must do exactly what you say you're going to do, otherwise the boundary is useless.

How to Stick to Your Boundaries & What to Do if They're Crossed

" Boundary setting helps you prioritize your needs over other people's wants."

– LAUREN KENSON

Once you set a boundary, you have to stick to it. There's no negotiation here.

Of course, sticking to your boundaries can be challenging, especially if you are used to putting other people's needs before your own. However, it's important to maintain your boundaries in order to establish a healthy and respectful relationship.

It's important to be clear from the start. When you have that conversation with your partner, or whoever you're setting a boundary with, make sure that you leave no room for confusion or blurred lines. In fact, ask if they have any questions, just to be sure.

Then, you should set consequences if the boundary is crossed. This might involve taking a break from the relationship (or friendship, whatever situation the boundary relates to), ending the relationship altogether, or simply communicating your disappointment or frustration.

And finally, be patient. Maintaining your boundaries can be a process, and it may take time to establish a healthy and respectful dynamic in your relationship. Be patient with yourself and your partner and focus on taking small steps towards your goals each day.

EXERCISE 19: How Can I Communicate My Boundaries?

Once you've worked out what boundaries you need to set, coming up with some ideas on how to communicate them can be tough. As a co-dependent person, this is going to be challenging for you, but you can do it! Here are some useful phrases you can use. Fill in the gaps with your boundaries and practice in the mirror.

I need to

....
....

I have a problem with

....
....

I have made a decision not to

....
....

I don't want to

....
....

I understand how you feel but I need

....
....

makes me uncomfortable.

I don't like it when you

....
....

It is important to me that

....

....

Who do you feel you need to set clear boundaries with? Write some notes below:

....
....
....
....
....
....
....
....
....
....

"Be a master at loving yourself and people will follow."

– KIM GUERRA

Chapter 5

It's Time to Focus on You

When you're co-dependent, you focus all your care and attention on other people. You give very little to yourself.

Why is that?

Do you believe it's selfish to focus on number one?

That couldn't be further from the truth.

It's not selfish – it's necessary for your well-being and personal growth. Here are some reasons why it's not selfish to focus on yourself. Memorize them for the next time you start feeling guilty for thinking about yourself.

> ❯ **You can't pour from an empty cup:** If you are constantly giving without taking care of yourself, you will eventually burn out. Focusing on yourself allows you to recharge and replenish your energy so you can continue giving.
> ❯ **You deserve to be happy:** Focusing on yourself means prioritizing your own happiness and well-being. This is not selfish, but a necessary part of living a fulfilling life.
> ❯ **You are responsible for your own life:** Ultimately, you are responsible for your own life and the choices you make.

Focusing on yourself means taking ownership of your life and making choices that align with your values and goals.

> **You can be a better partner, friend, and family member:** When you focus on yourself, you become a better version of yourself. This allows you to be a better partner, friend, and family member, as you are able to show up fully and authentically in your relationships.

> **You can inspire others:** When you focus on yourself and prioritize your own growth and well-being, you can inspire others to do the same. This can have a positive ripple effect on those around you.

When you focus on yourself, you start loving who you are. You focus on your strengths and not your weaknesses, and you realize that you're worth a whole lot more than you originally thought. However, there is a difference between self-care and going a little too far.

Let's explore that.

EXERCISE 20: Self-Care Vs Selfishness

This exercise should help clear up any lingering doubts about self-care, and help you see that it's not selfish at all. Of course, if you take it too far, it can be, but by focusing on your personal needs, you won't cross that line.

Read the questions below and choose the answer you feel fits best. Don't think too much, just opt for your first response.

1. You cancel plans with a friend because you're feeling overwhelmed and need some alone time. Is this an example of self-care or selfishness?

   a) Self-care
   b) Selfishness

2. You refuse to help a family member with a problem because you don't want to be inconvenienced. Is this an example of self-care or selfishness?

   a) Self-care
   b) Selfishness

3. You take a day off work to rest and recharge. Is this an example of self-care or selfishness?

   a) Self-care
   b) Selfishness

4. You spend money on a spa day to relax and unwind. Is this an example of self-care or selfishness?

   a) Self-care
   b) Selfishness

5. You prioritize your own needs and desires over your partner's. Is this an example of self-care or selfishness?

   a) Self-care
   b) Selfishness

6. You set boundaries with a friend who is constantly taking advantage of your kindness. Is this an example of self-care or selfishness?

   a) Self-care
   b) Selfishness

7. You refuse to compromise or make sacrifices in your relationships. Is this an example of self-care or selfishness?

   a) Self-care
   b) Selfishness

Answers:

1. A - Self-care
2. B - Selfishness
3. A - Self-care
4. A - Self-care
5. B - Selfish

Once you understand the importance of self-care, you can start working on yourself, feel a whole lot better, and you'll be able to develop equal relationships in the future.

What Should You Do More Of?

" Love yourself so much that when someone treats you wrong, you recognize it."

— RENA ROSE

Self-care includes things like making sure that you are getting enough sleep, eating healthy, nutritious food but remembering to have treats occasionally, exercising, spending time with people who build you up, setting goals, and indulging in the things that make you feel good.

💡 EXERCISE 21: Give Me More!

So, what do you think you need to do more of? Write them down in the space below.

....
....
....
....
....
....

Now, it's time to work out how you're going to fit those things into your life. This shouldn't be tough, as these things are your new priorities. If you have to move other things to fit them in, do so. Scribble your ideas below:

....
....
....
....
....
....
....
....

EXERCISE 22: Find Some Enjoyable Things to Do

You may not know what your hobbies are, or you can't think of anything that you used to enjoy so much that fits in with your life and your personality right now. In that case, here's some inspiration.

Check the table below and circle anything that you'd like to make a regular part of your life.

Going for a walk	Looking after a pet	Going for coffee with a friend
Learning to bake or cook	Taking nieces/nephews out for ice cream	Having a well-deserved daytime nap
Reading a good book	Catching up on Netflix shows	Getting a massage
Getting nails/hair done	Listening to your favorite music	Learning a new language

If you see something that you'd like to do more of, circle it and make it a regular part of your life. No excuses, just do it!

Recognizing Stress

It's very easy to become chronically stressed when you're co-dependent. Here's why:

> Over-responsibility:

Codependent individuals focus predominantly on their partner's needs. They are so focused on anticipating and fulfilling their partner's needs that they never realize that they are stretching themselves too thin. They rarely find time to relax and take care of themselves, as they find this selfish. Co-dependent individuals are too focused on the people around them, the people they depend on for validation, that they don't seem to realize the stress building in their body.

Taking responsibility for another person is stressful, mainly because their actions, reactions, and choices are beyond our control. However, co-dependent individuals falsely believe that they have control over the other person, and any event that makes it seem that they've lost control drives them over the edge. The frustration compounds and stress builds, and because there's no healthy outlet, the stress snowballs.

> **Lack of boundaries:**

Codependent individuals find it difficult to say "no" to their partners requests and demands. They believe that denying the request makes it likely that their partner will leave them because their needs are not fulfilled. However, this unfettered access to their time, resources, and energy leaves them drained, unable to adopt healthy coping skills when they are stressed. Healthy boundaries serve to keep us safe from exploitation, but because co-dependent individuals have a flawed perception of boundaries, they are always open to their partners. Even when they are tired and overwhelmed, they allow more things to be piled on their plate.

Additionally, co-dependent individuals have a hard time expressing their emotions, and these repressed emotions further compound their stress.

> **Emotional rollercoaster:**

Because they take responsibility for their partner's emotions and actions or lack thereof, co-dependent individuals shoulder more than their own share of challenges. In a bid to anticipate their partners' needs, deal with their partners' emotions, and process their own emotions, they find themselves scrambling to figure out what they are experiencing in any moment. They get bogged down by their partners' sour moods, feel elated when their partners are in a good mood, and find themselves conflicted when they cannot interpret their partners' emotions.

Extreme emotional states are stressful for any individual, and these constant emotional highs and lows mean that co-dependent individuals are always under stress. The accumulation of these emotional reactions means that the stress is never properly mitigated, and it builds up to chronic levels over time.

> **Neglecting self-care:**

Codependent individuals tend to put their own wellbeing on the backburner, choosing to focus their attention on their partner. They sacrifice their wellbeing just to keep their partner happy, which means that they never take the time to address their own needs and wants. With the focus solely on the other person, co-dependent individuals never develop the necessary skills to deal with stress in a healthy manner. They look to their partners to solve their problems, or they choose to repress their emotions and drown their sorrows in less healthy ways, like drugs and alcohol.

Because they've never taken the time to check in with themselves, self-care is essentially nonexistent. This means that stress relief is never a priority, and they remain in the state of agitation until things boil over. Self-care is about finding ways or releasing pent-up energy, emotions, and frustrations – something co-dependent individuals never undertake.

> **Inability to cope:**

Co-dependent individuals usually fail to develop the necessary coping skills to deal with the challenges they face. They repress their emotions, blame others for the predicament they're in (usually their partners), or deal with their frustrations in unhealthy ways. This means that their stresses are rarely addressed properly, and they build up over time and become overwhelming.

Now, I don't need to tell you that stress is bad for you, right?

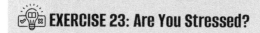 EXERCISE 23: Are You Stressed?

How many of these statements do you agree with?

- I feel tired all the time.
- I have trouble sleeping or staying asleep.
- I feel irritable or easily frustrated.
- I have trouble concentrating or making decisions.
- I feel overwhelmed by my responsibilities.
- I don't have enough time for myself.
- I feel like I'm constantly on edge or anxious.
- I don't enjoy things that used to bring me pleasure.
- I feel like I'm just going through the motions.
- I have physical symptoms like headaches or stomachaches.
- I feel like I'm not doing anything well.
- I feel like I'm running on empty.

- I have trouble relaxing or unwinding.
- I feel like I'm always behind or playing catch-up.
- I feel like I'm not living up to my own expectations.
- I feel like I'm not living up to others' expectations.
- I feel like I'm not appreciated or valued.
- I feel like I'm stuck in a rut or routine.
- I feel like I'm not making progress in my life.
- I feel like I'm not in control of my life.

If you agree with more than two of these statements, it may be a sign that you're experiencing stress or burnout. It's important to take steps to manage your stress and prioritize self-care in order to prevent burnout and maintain your well-being.

So, how can you do that?

> **Practice relaxation techniques:** Relaxation techniques such as deep breathing, meditation, yoga, or tai chi can help calm your mind and reduce stress.

> **Exercise regularly:** Exercise releases endorphins, which are natural mood-boosters that can help reduce stress. Aim for at least 30 minutes of physical activity most days of the week.

> **Get enough sleep:** Lack of sleep can contribute to stress and anxiety. Aim for 7-9 hours of sleep each night and establish a consistent sleep routine.

> **Eat a healthy diet:** Eating a diet rich in fruits, vegetables, whole grains, and lean protein can help reduce stress and promote overall health.

> **Practice time management:** Prioritize your tasks and responsibilities, and break them down into smaller, manageable steps. This can help reduce feelings of overwhelm and stress.

> **Connect with others:** Talking to friends, family, or a therapist can help reduce stress and provide a sense of support and connection.

> **Practice self-care:** Engage in activities that bring you joy and relaxation, such as reading a book, taking a bath, or listening to music.

> **Avoid unhealthy coping mechanisms:** Avoid using alcohol, drugs, or other unhealthy coping mechanisms to deal with stress.

Which of these points do you need to work on the most? Write them down here, including a few ideas on how you can do that.

....
....
....
....
....
....
....

The Art of Saying "No"

> "To love yourself right now just as you are, is to give yourself heaven. Don't wait until you die. If you wait, you die now. If you love, you live now."
>
> – ALAN COHEN

As a person who is used to being co-dependent, saying "no" will be something that makes you feel very uncomfortable at first. But if you continue saying "yes" to everything, how are you ever going to have any time for yourself?

And remember, time for yourself is important too!

Saying "no" is something you need to practice, and it will feel wrong to you for a while but keep at it.

Why? Well, learning to say no is important for several reasons:

> **Protecting your time and energy:**

  Saying "yes" all the time leaves no room for you to spend your time and energy in ways that will benefit you. You are always caught up in other people's - including your partner's - demands, requests, and needs. This means that you leave no time for yourself, and you're left stretched too thin and exhausted. Saying "no" is the first step in reclaiming your time and energy and spending them on things that matter to you.

> **Setting boundaries:**

  Saying "no" is one of the most effective ways of communicating your boundaries. While the first "no" will undoubtedly be difficult, you have to start somewhere. Setting boundaries is not about coming up with a list of rules and regulations. It can be as simple as refusing to take a break with your coworker until you've completed your predetermined agenda. It is saying "no" to your partner when they want to go out on a weeknight and you have an early morning.

In the long run your boundaries will be clearer, but as you're starting out, getting comfortable with saying "no" should be your priority.

> **Honoring your commitments:**

When you say "yes" to things that you had not planned on indulging in, you take away time for the things that were in your schedule. You cannot be in two places at once, and multitasking is not as efficient as we think it is. So, if you say yes to going out with your partner on a random Tuesday night, you sacrifice your sleep. When you choose to do someone else's work, you fail to complete your own.

Saying "no" allows you to stay true to your priorities. And even if you don't necessarily say "no," you cannot jump into fulfilling anyone's request without first evaluating what you'll be giving up. When you remain true to your priorities and commitments, you show up for yourself. You build trust in your ability to stand up for yourself, which gives you the boost to keep protecting yourself.

> **Building self-respect:**

Saying "yes" all the time breaks you down. Many people who find it difficult to say no always wish they could, mainly because becoming a doormat negatively impacts their self-esteem and self-respect. It is difficult to respect yourself when you cannot be assertive or protect your time and energy. However, as you learn to say "no" and follow through on the promises you made to yourself, you develop a sense of appreciation for your strength.

As you become more comfortable with prioritizing your needs and ideals, you feel more confident in your capabilities, and your self-respect builds.

> **Encouraging respect from others:**

   When you start enforcing your boundaries, you will attract pushback from the people who were taking advantage of your inability to say "no." However, as you enforce your boundaries and stay true to yourself, others always seem to get in line. They understand where the line is drawn, and they start respecting your ability to follow through on your own plans.

   However, as a co-dependent person, you need to be careful about falling back into your old patterns. As you gain respect from others, don't revel in the validation and start seeking it out. Remind yourself why you chose to start saying "no."

EXERCISE 24: When It's Okay to Say "No"

Now, learning how to say "no" doesn't mean that you go around refusing to do anything at all! Instead, you need to assess how you feel, and if you truly don't want to do something, can't, or don't have time, just say "no!"

Let's practice a little. In these scenarios, when do you think it's okay to say "no?"

Scenario 1: Your boss asks you to do an urgent task because you're the only one with prior experience in that particular area. You're busy already.

Should you say no? Write down your thoughts:

....

....

....

....

....

Answer – You probably can't say "no" outright in this situation, but you can explain to your boss that you already have a heavy workload and ask if some of that can be taken off so you can focus on the urgent task.

***

Scenario 2: Your friend asks you to go to their house because they want you to help them prepare for a job interview the next day. You're on a date night with your partner and you promised each other you wouldn't cancel unless it was urgent.

Should you say no? Write down your thoughts:

....

....

....

....

....

Answer – In this situation, you can say "no," but you can say that you're happy to look over what they've done the next day. You should prioritize your relationship in certain situations and if you've both committed to date nights once a week, that should be a priority.

***

Scenario 3: A colleague at work asks you to collaborate with them on a project. You have worked with this person before, and you know that they often don't do their share of the work and take credit for ideas that aren't their own.

Should you say no? Write down your thoughts:

....
....
....
....
....

Answer – You can absolutely say "no." You don't have to tell them that you don't trust them and that they're lazy; instead, you can say that you're busy on other projects and wish them luck.

Now can you see how saying "no" is a self-preservation strategy that helps you handle difficult requests with ease? Choose your battles wisely, but never feel pushed into doing something you truly don't want to do just because you're trying to please another person.

Those days are over!

"The only person who can change your life is you."

– UNKNOWN

Chapter 6

Five Steps to Break Free From Co-dependency

Your life is your own. Other people may enhance your life and bring you joy, but in the end, you are the only person who can truly make it beautiful.

The last five chapters have helped you understand what co-dependence is, why it's a negative habit, how you can examine the reasons behind it, and what you can do to change. Now, we need to focus on the exact steps. So, that's what this chapter is: a recap and deep dive into the five steps you need to take.

Remember, self-care should be your priority. Other people are important, but your life doesn't revolve around them. The only person who will be with you from the moment you're born until the day you die is you. So, doesn't it make sense to please yourself more often?

Step 1 – Recognize & Acknowledge The Problem

This is pretty much already done. By getting this far, you know you have a problem with co-dependence, right? Otherwise, why would you have picked up this book and read almost to the end?

The first step in breaking free from co-dependence is to recognize and acknowledge that there is a problem. This might involve reflecting on your behavior and relationships, and identifying patterns of behavior that are unhealthy or dysfunctional.

One of those issues is understanding how specific situations create heightened emotional responses. In the end, your emotions power your co-dependent behavior, and these are linked to triggers. We've already spent some time thinking about your triggers, but how about dealing with emotions that might be hard to handle in the moment?

Let's take a quiz and see how you tend to deal with these emotional problems.

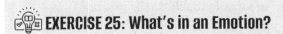 EXERCISE 25: What's in an Emotion?

If I ask you to describe your response to heightened emotions, you'll probably struggle to answer. After all, different emotions evoke different responses. This quiz will give you greater insight.

1. When you're feeling anxious or stressed, what do you usually do?

    a) Try to distract myself by doing something else
    b) Talk to someone about how I'm feeling
    c) Exercise or do something physical to release the tension
    d) Panic and lash out at others

2. How do you typically react when someone criticizes you or disagrees with you?

    a) Get defensive and argue back
    b) Shut down and withdraw from the conversation
    c) Try to understand their perspective and have a calm discussion

d) Feel hurt and upset, but keep my thoughts to myself

3. When you're feeling overwhelmed, what helps you feel more in control?

a) Making a to-do list or schedule to organize my thoughts
b) Taking a break and doing something enjoyable or relaxing
c) Talking to someone about my feelings and getting support
d) Withdrawing without explanation

4. How do you usually express your anger or frustration?

a) Yell or lash out at others
b) Internalize my feelings and don't express them
c) Use "I" statements to express my feelings calmly and assertively
d) Use humor or sarcasm to diffuse the situation

5. When you're feeling sad or down, what helps you feel better?

a) Keeping busy and distracting myself from my feelings
b) Talking to someone about how I'm feeling
c) Doing something creative or expressive, like writing or painting
d) Replaying the reasons why I feel sad

Scoring:

For each question, give yourself one point for answer (c) and half a point for answer (b). Give yourself zero points for answer (a) and (d).

Results:

- **0-1 points:** You may struggle with managing your emotions and could benefit from seeking support or learning coping strategies.

- **1.5-2.5 points:** You have some effective strategies for managing your emotions but may benefit from further developing your skills.

- **3-4 points:** You have strong emotional regulation skills and can effectively manage your emotions in most situations.

- **4.5-5 points:** You have excellent emotional regulation skills and can navigate challenging emotions with ease.

Taking a moment to breathe and calm down before reacting is the best way to handle any extreme emotion. If you don't do this, you risk jumping in feet first, and then whatever you say or do can't be taken back.

So, the next time something bothers you:

- Stop
- Close your eyes for a second
- Take a deep breath in through your nose for a slow count of three
- Hold the breath for a count of two
- Exhale through your mouth for a slow count of three
- Repeat until you have calmed down sufficiently to think about your next move.

Step 2 – Truly Understand Co-dependency

This is another item you can tick off your list! That's exactly what you've been doing by reading this book. But if you're still unclear or unsure about any element of co-dependency, remember that you can go back and re-read any sections. This workbook will always be there for you.

You can take it a step further and read some articles or blogs about co-dependence, so you see that you're not the only person to deal with this problem. Group therapy sessions could help if you feel you need to go down that route, but remember, you can seek support in your loved ones too. But first, you need to open up to them.

> **EXERCISE 26: Who Do You Miss?**

Use the space below to write a list of people you don't see very much anymore because you've spent too much time focusing on your partner or a particular person. Then, scribble down how you can try to reconnect with them.

....
....
....
....
....
....
....

Step 3 - Set Positive Boundaries

> "Knowing you are becoming someone you can be proud of ... there is no greater motivation than that."
>
> – UNKNOWN

This should be pretty clear already, seeing as we did a whole chapter on it. But remember, boundaries are your way of saying, "hey, that's not okay with me." There is nothing wrong with telling people what you do and don't want; it's part of a healthy relationship. But remember that they can do the same with you, and you need to listen and respond accordingly.

But it's not only partners you need to set boundaries with. It can be anyone in your life who does something that makes you feel uncomfortable. For instance, your parents may be extremely nosey and want to know every single aspect of your life. This might make you feel suffocated. It's not wrong to ask them to back off a little, but obviously, you need to do so in a respectful way.

Maybe your colleague talks constantly throughout the day, and you can't get your work done. You could set a boundary by asking them not to talk to you when they can clearly see you're concentrating. Tell them you're more than happy to sit and chat with them at lunch.

Perhaps your friend is over-familiar with your partner, and it makes you very uncomfortable. In that case, it's totally within your rights to ask them to maintain a respectful distance with your partner and to respect your relationship. After all, they wouldn't want you to do the same with their partner, would they?

If people don't like your boundaries, that's not your problem. However, you should keep the following points in mind:

> **Be clear and firm:** Make sure your boundaries are clear and specific and communicate them in a firm but respectful way. It's important to be consistent and stick to your boundaries, even if someone disagrees with them.

> **Validate their feelings:** It's possible that the person may feel upset or frustrated with your boundaries, and it's important to validate their feelings while still maintaining your boundaries. You can acknowledge their feelings and express

empathy, but remain clear about your own needs and boundaries.

> **Compromise if possible:** If there's room for compromise, you can try to find a solution that works for both parties. However, it's important to make sure that any compromise still respects your own boundaries and needs.

> **Seek support:** If the person continues to push back against your boundaries or becomes aggressive or abusive, it's important to seek support from a trusted friend, family member, or professional. They can provide you with emotional support and help you develop strategies for dealing with the situation.

Remember, setting boundaries is an important part of taking care of yourself and establishing healthy relationships. While it's possible that not everyone will agree with, or respect, your boundaries, it's important to stay true to your own needs and values, no matter how difficult it may be.

A person who doesn't want to respect your boundaries or refuses to hear them isn't someone who cares about you that much. It's a hard pill to swallow, but it's the unfortunate truth.

EXERCISE 27: Pinpointing My Boundaries

Use the table below to clearly identify the healthy and unhealthy boundaries in your relationship, including the ones you want to implement, and what you can do about them right now. This action plan will help you to move forward with a positive mindset!

Healthy Boundaries Currently in My Relationship(S)	How Can I Make Them Better
Unhealthy Boundaries I Can Identify in My Relationship(S)	How I Can Make Them Better

Step 4 - Practice Self-Care Regularly

Remember our mantra from earlier? Say it with me: "self-care isn't selfish!"

But how much self-care do you currently do, and is there space for more? In my opinion, there's always space for more, but let's see what your starting point is.

EXERCISE 28: Do You Take Enough (Self) Care?

Answer the following questions, and remember to be honest!

1. How often do you take time to relax and recharge?

    a) Almost never
    b) Occasionally
    c) Regularly
    d) Every day

2. How often do you engage in physical activity or exercise?

    a) Almost never
    b) Occasionally
    c) Regularly
    d) Every day

3. How often do you eat healthy, nutritious foods?

    a) Almost never
    b) Occasionally
    c) Regularly
    d) Every day

4. How often do you engage in activities that bring you joy and fulfilment?

    a) Almost never
    b) Occasionally
    c) Regularly
    d) Every day

5. How often do you practice mindfulness or meditation?

    a) Almost never
    b) Occasionally
    c) Regularly
    d) Every day

6. How often do you connect with loved ones or friends?

a) Almost never
b) Occasionally
c) Regularly
d) Every day

7. How often do you get enough sleep?

a) Almost never
b) Occasionally
c) Regularly
d) Every day

Scoring:

For each question, give yourself one point for answer (d), half a point for answer (c), zero points for answer (b), and minus one point for answer (a).

Results:

- 7 to -3 points: You may be neglecting important self-care elements and could benefit from prioritizing your own needs and well-being.

- 2 to 2 points: You have some areas of self-care that you could focus on improving, but you are generally taking care of yourself.

- 2.5 to 5 points: You have a good balance of self-care elements and are taking care of yourself well.

- 5.5 to 7 points: You are prioritizing your self-care and taking care of yourself in all the important areas.

Self-care is something you need to start doing right now; no excuses, no delays. I mentioned the idea of a full day of self-care, and I think that's something everyone should do. You might have heard of 'Self-Care Sunday'; well, it doesn't have to be a Sunday, it can be any day.

EXERCISE 29: Plan Your Perfect Day

Let's plan out your day of total and utter self-care:

Nominated day: ....

A few favorite foods I might like:

....

....

....

....

A few activities I might enjoy:

....

....

....

....

....

Self-care day promises I make to myself:

....

....

....

....

....

....

It's best if you spend your self-care day alone; that way you can really focus on yourself, but if you want other people to join you, that's fine too – it's your day! However, make sure you don't get sucked into doing things they want to do, and putting your own needs at the bottom of the list again. Hello, co-dependence!

Step 5 - Seeking Help & Support

> "Never underestimate the power you have to take your life in a new direction."
>
> — GERMANY KENT

Breaking free from co-dependence can be challenging, and it's important to seek support from others. This might involve talking to friends or family members, joining a support group, or working with a therapist.

But sometimes, the best support you can give is to yourself. When your emotions rise and you're about to engage in co-dependent behaviors, self-soothing can be a fantastic way forward. That way, you avoid going down the same road, the one that has never served you well, and you come out the other side feeling positive.

This is called self-soothing. So, what is your self-soothing style?

Let's find out.

EXERCISE 30: How Do You Self-Soothe?

Think carefully before answering the following questions. Go with the option that best fits your preference.

1. When you're feeling stressed or anxious, what do you typically do?

   a) Exercise or engage in physical activity
   b) Listen to music or podcasts
   c) Take a bath or shower
   d) Write in a journal or talk to a friend

2. When you're feeling overwhelmed, what helps you feel more grounded?

   a) Spending time in nature or going for a walk
   b) Practicing mindfulness or meditation
   c) Engaging in a creative activity, such as painting or drawing
   d) Watching a favorite movie or TV show

3. When you're feeling sad or down, what helps lift your mood?

   a) Engaging in physical activity, such as running or dancing
   b) Spending time with friends or family
   c) Listening to music or reading a book
   d) Engaging in a self-care activity, such as getting a massage or taking a nap

4. When you're feeling angry or frustrated, what helps you calm down?

a) A. Taking deep breaths or practicing relaxation techniques
b) B. Engaging in a physical activity, such as boxing or weightlifting
c) C. Writing in a journal or talking to a therapist
d) D. Engaging in a creative activity, such as painting or drawing

5. When you're feeling overwhelmed by work or responsibilities, what helps you feel more organized and in control?

a) Making a to-do list or breaking tasks down into smaller steps
b) Practicing time management techniques, such as the Pomodoro method
c) Engaging in a creative activity, such as bullet journaling or scrapbooking
d) Asking for help or delegating tasks to others

Answers:

- If you answered mostly A's, your ideal self-soothing method may involve physical activity or exercise.
- If you answered mostly B's, mindfulness or meditation may be your ideal self-soothing method.
- If you answered mostly C's, listening to music or engaging in a creative activity may be your ideal self-soothing method.

- If you answered mostly D's, talking to a friend or engaging in a self-care activity may be your ideal self-soothing method.

Remember, everyone is different, and what works for one person may not work for everyone. What you can do, however, is find the option that fits you best, and then whenever you need to calm yourself down or you simply want to feel better, you know what to do!

"Happiness is not something you postpone for the future; it is something you design for the present."

– JIM ROHN

Conclusion

You've reached the end of the workbook, pat yourself on the back for a job well done!

This book will help you finally say goodbye to your co-dependent ways and learn how to be self-sufficient and happy again. You'll have much better relationships, and you'll find people who care about your wellbeing, not those who walk all over you because you've allowed them to do so for so long.

You should be feeling proud of yourself right now. I'm proud of you!

So, what have you learned? Use the space below to scribble down the points that stood out for you during your journey through this workbook:

....

....

....

....

....

....

....

Understanding co-dependency is the first step on your journey to freedom. Once you know what to look for, why it happens, and acknowledge that you've fallen foul of it yourself, you're already one step ahead.

In the end, it all comes down to fear. Fear of not being enough, fear of being alone, fear of being rejected, fear of abandonment, fear of someone seeing the real you… the list goes on.

But do you know what? There is nothing to be afraid of. You are enough, you're never alone because you have your friends, family, and yourself; if someone rejects you, so what! Reject them back! The right ones will never abandon you, and don't be scared of showing someone the raw, authentic version of you. It's wonderful, and they should feel grateful they get to see it.

You're not alone in this. So many people have struggled with co-dependency in the past, but it's entirely possible to kick it out of your life and look forward to a brighter future.

You now have all the tools you need to do exactly that. All you need to do now is show willingness and effort to work through it and come out the other side much stronger.

EXERCISE 31: Are You Ready to Recover?

Just how far have you come? Are you ready to change your life and move on? This quiz will give you all the answers you need.

Are you willing to take responsibility for your own actions and emotions?

- a) Yes, I believe in owning my own behavior and emotions
- b) No, I feel like others are responsible for my behavior and emotions
- c) Sometimes, depending on the situation
- d) I don't know

Are you willing to seek support from others, such as a therapist or support group?

- a) Yes, I believe in the power of seeking support from others
- b) No, I feel like I should be able to handle things on my own
- c) Sometimes, depending on the situation
- d) I don't know

Are you willing to set boundaries and prioritize your own needs?

- a) Yes, I believe in the importance of setting boundaries and prioritizing my own needs
- b) No, I feel like I have to put others first in order to be a good person
- c) Sometimes, depending on the situation
- d) I don't know

Are you willing to let go of relationships or behaviors that are harmful or no longer serving you?

    a) Yes, I believe in the importance of letting go of things that are no longer serving me
    b) No, I feel like I need to hold onto things to feel secure
    c) Sometimes, depending on the situation
    d) I don't know

Are you willing to practice self-care and prioritize your own well-being?

    a) Yes, I believe in the importance of self-care and prioritizing my own well-being
    b) No, I feel like I don't have time or energy for self-care
    c) Sometimes, depending on the situation
    d) I don't know

If you answered mostly (a) to these questions, it is a sign that you are ready to recover from co-dependence. Great news! However, it's important to remember that recovery is a process that takes time and effort. But I know you can do it!

> "Learn from yesterday, live for today, hope for the future."
>
> — ALBERT EINSTEIN

Don't beat yourself up about your past mistakes. They're done; there's nothing you can do except learn from them. But learning is a gift. Our experiences give us everything we need to move on and make the rest of our lives better. And you might have a lot of learning to do, but that means your life is going to be amazing once you've worked it all out!

Conclusion

Look, people come into our lives and they either stick around or they leave. There is nothing you can do to control it. You can't hold onto them so tight by doing everything they want hoping they'll stay. That's not genuine. You want people to stay because they want to, not because they're so comfortable taking advantage of a good thing.

So, it's time to make a vow. From today, you will no longer put everyone in front of yourself. You are worthy. You are strong. And you are more deserving of love than you realize.

All you need to do now is go out and put all the advice I've given you into action.

Your life is going to be fantastic. You just have to believe it.

Made in the USA
Middletown, DE
14 September 2023